MAXIMIZE INFLUENCE

HOW TO BE THE INFLUENCER ~~NOT THE INFLUENCED~~

INFLUENCED  INFLUENCER

CHASE KREGER

Cover Design: Chase Kreger & Stephanie Popham

Cover Image: Shutterstock Images

Printed in the United States of America

First Printing Edition, 2021

ISBN (Paperback): 978-1-09839-565-0

To My Dad

If you were here with us, you wouldn't need to read this book. You already lived it.

Thank you for teaching me about influence. Over the years, I have only found one Influencer better than you. The words on the following pages are an effort to describe the pictures you both painted.

I love you.

CONTENTS

CHAPTER 5: CULTURE

CHAPTER 6: LEARNING

CHAPTER 7: SERVING

CONCLUSION: WE ARE HERE

NOTES

ABOUT THE AUTHOR

ABOUT MAXIMIZE VALUE

ADDITIONAL RESOURCES

INTRODUCTION

---

maximize: *make as* large or *great as possible.*

influence: the capacity to have an effect on *the character*, development, or behavior *of someone* or something.

WHY ANOTHER BOOK?

Modern society, and modern media is completely infused with meaningless communication that removes any depth of importance. If we allow it, our thoughts will be corrupted with worthless ideas, and unedited opinions, all of which are fighting for our uninterrupted focus and attention. They are vying for our time, energy, belief, and response. They are trying to *influence* us.

This oversaturation of information creates a reality that life begins to lose its meaning and we suddenly lose discernment of what is valuable. With regard for this new reality, I must ask: Do we really need another book? No.

Instead, we need a book that captivates us to escape the disorienting, constant noise of our society so that we might be able to discern what is good, what is noble, what is virtuous, and what is true. If we were to find such a book, we may be able to find ourselves in a place where we have something of merit to say and something valuable to give to another. Instead of being influenced by the blasphemous culture that surrounds us, we might be able to demonstrate positive influence in the face of such adversity. This is the aim of the book you have in your hands.

WHY INFLUENCE?

Influence impacts every person on this planet. No matter who you are or what you do, you are trying to influence someone or something. It doesn't matter whether you see yourself as an influencer or not, your ability or inability to influence yourself and influence others will affect every area of your life. It will also, in many ways, determine how much you are able to positively impact people.

We, as influencers, are not just teaching the techniques of leading and selling. We are teaching the techniques of a new and better way of life. We are teaching people how to care, how to love, and how to have better relationships. We are helping people open the doors to more friendships, more self-confidence, more courage, and more freedom. Being an influencer, when done properly, is the most noble of work. No other work yields the deep rewards that come from helping people be their best.

HOW THIS BOOK WAS WRITTEN

Target Audience (1): To the one who wonders if you were created for more, if you should focus on helping people, if you should be an influencer – this book was written for you. And the answer is yes, three times.

Target Audience (2): This book was also written to myself. If it sounds like advice, it is advice to myself to do something more intentionally, more consistently, or more frequently. Also, I believe George Orwell was speaking the truth when he said... "If people cannot write well, they cannot think well. And if they cannot think well, others will do their thinking for them." I am my own target audience ultimately because I refuse to let others do my thinking for me.

Curation: I'm convinced that whenever you think your idea is unique, you simply haven't read widely enough on that subject. I know this to be true about this book. The main ideas in this book have been curated and synthesized over the course of more than three decades. Some of these ideas have been formed from experiencing, reading, watching, writing, praying, doing, listening, and teaching. This particular book has been constructed by linking several of my personal experiences, and several previously disconnected ideas, all of which relate to influence.

Author: One thing is for sure, the author of this book is far from perfect. Just because I know these truths does not mean I apply them flawlessly. That said, I can assure you that the truths in this book have been tried and tested, and they work. I can also assure you that I do not know the comprehensive recipe of influence, but the topics in this book are a few of the non-negotiable ingredients within the recipe.

Assumptions: Many authors assume that their readers are unintelligent. Thus, they feel the need to connect the dots and do all the interpretation for their audience. I've made the opposite assumption. I assume you are brilliant, and you can connect your own dots. You can interpret the conversation for yourself. That's why you won't see a ton of context after each story or example. The example teaches itself, and you can do the interpretation yourself.

Time Frame: I started writing this book back in 2014 and I finished the first version back in 2016. Then I ripped it all up and threw it all in the trash. I proceeded to repeat some version of that process two more times. This is technically the fourth version of this book, and it is still incomplete. But, deadlines can be a great motivator. And as they say, books leave behind a record of where the author is in that particular moment in time. So, in this moment of time, I have given much as I can and I hope you enjoy.

WHY READ THIS BOOK?

Why should we keep reading books? Why should we consistently revisit the same ideas? Because that is exactly what we all need. Triggers to remind us of how to be better. How to improve. How to help others.

We all have a core problem when our heads rise from the pillow each morning. The problem is not that the prior information we've consumed is useless, it is that our ability to focus is transient. We can't possibly focus on one idea all the time, but we can be intentional about consumption and refocusing our minds. That's another reason why these words are on these pages.

FORMAT OF THE BOOK

In each of the seven main chapters you will find:
- Chapter Title & Favorite Quote on the Subject
- Three Things to Unlearn
- Three Things to Learn
- Chapter Summary

FINAL THOUGHTS

I've heard several authors say that most of a book is fluff, and only a small percentage of the book has anything important to say. In my experience over the last decade, I believe that statement to be accurate. While that may be the unfortunate reality, I know for a fact that some books are outliers, and here's to hoping the one in your hands is an outlier for you.

And finally, I pray that these words would captivate you to flee from the normalcies of being *influenced* by the degeneracy of our culture and provoke you to develop the courage and boldness needed to live the *influential* life that you were created to live. Amen.

CHAPTER I

PARADIGMS

"Do not conform to the patterns in this world, but be

transformed by the renewing of your mind."

– Paul of Tarsus

UNLEARN NARCISSISM

August 22, 2012. It was a Wednesday evening a little after 5PM. The leaves were just getting ready to change colors, not a cloud in the sky, the sun was shining brightly, and it felt like one-hundred degrees outside. I was by myself, waiting for my friend Jared Miller to arrive at our ministry house on 3rd Street in Louisville. Less than a mile from Churchill Downs.

At that moment, I found myself in the backyard staring down at a broken flash drive that was crushed into a thousand pieces...

With a hammer in my hand.

I remember it vividly. I remember almost everything from that month of my life. Nine days prior my Dad moved to heaven. He was out on a run at Strawtown Koteewi Park in Noblesville, Indiana. He had a massive heart attack and moved quickly from this life to the next. We never got to say goodbye to our best friend. That happened on Monday, August 13, 2012. He was 51 years young and we were devastated.

I returned to work on the following Monday and on Tuesday I had to go through a presentation training course where we delivered several different presentations, which were recorded on camera and stored on that (broken) flash drive. All while twelve people got to watch you. It was sobering.

Shaking nervously, both with my hands and my voice. Sweating. Red blotches all over my cheeks and my neck. On camera, I watched myself moving anxiously with no purpose. Nothing eloquent came out of my mouth for the entire day. I even remember messing up my name when I was introducing myself. It was truly that bad and I'm not embellishing this story. I hated every minute of the entire experience, and that was just the first day.

After day one, I went home and spent the night prepping, planning, and practicing. I really worked hard to improve myself so I could come back the next day with more poise and confidence. Like an alcoholic who just drank his last drink, I was done with sucking at presentations.

The next day, I showed up enthusiastic and ready to go, and wouldn't you believe it? Day two was worse than day one. I remember being up at the podium and literally freezing in front of everyone. I didn't even finish that particular presentation nor did I watch the recording of it. I removed myself from the podium and walked out of the room quicker than the trainer could initiate a mandatory half-hearted clap for me.

I wasn't sad and I didn't cry... Most of the week prior was spent in tears. At that moment in time, I was frustrated, and not about my Dad dying. It was frustrating because this may have been the first truly paradoxical experience in my life. It probably wasn't the first paradoxical moment of my life, but it was first time I can remember thinking that this doesn't make any sense.

Here's the backstory... Throughout my entire life, I was told to work hard and focus on improving myself. So I did, and it worked. If I wanted to improve at sports, I practiced harder and got better. If I wanted to get good grades, I just focused on improving myself, and got better grades. You name it, and focusing on improving myself was the answer that always satisfied.

Until that smoking hot day in August of 2012. "Why do I suck at this?" I asked myself. It wasn't maddening to be bad at presenting, being bad at stuff is a daily experience. It was infuriating to work so hard to improve myself and it wasn't fixing the problem. Math always makes sense, and this wasn't adding up.

Then, the next moment, with the hammer in my hand, the lightbulb hit me like the bricks hit Marv in *Home Alone 2: Lost in New York*. As I was waiting for Jared to arrive at the house so we could start the renovation work in the laundry room, I sat down in my navy blue 2001 Volvo S40 and I turned on a song by my favorite artist of all-time (Sean Cates). Here are the penetrating lyrics that shifted my paradigm:

"BACK IN THE DAILY MY LIFE WAS SELF. LIVING THIS LIFE, I DIDN'T LIKE TO FAIL. BUT THAT IS JUST WHAT YOU WILL DO IF YOU LIVE THIS LIFE JUST FOR YOU."

Boom. Fireworks went off in my brain and it all started to make sense again. In presentations, and in life, when you want to maximize influence, your focus needs to be on helping others, not helping yourself. That truth, perhaps, is the most remarkable thing about presentations. It is impossible to be great if you focus on yourself. The only way to the destination of presentation excellence is to focus on serving your audience.

When you deliver presentations for a living, you realize that most people don't care about you. They care about what you can do for them. In other words, presentations aren't about the presenter, they are all about them. If we want to maximize influence, the only appropriate starting point is to focus on them.

We will begin to win as soon we help others win...

AND HELPING OTHERS WIN IS NOT JUST THE STARTING POINT FOR VICTORY, IT IS THE BEST POSSIBLE VICTORY.

Selah.

UNLEARN ENTITLEMENT

In the previous story, I felt entitled to a certain result if I applied the correct formula. That, believe it or not, leads us perfectly into the next paradigm we need to unlearn.

You are about to read something that is, for some reason, highly controversial in our world today. Brace yourself…

LIFE IS WHAT YOU MAKE OF IT

Yes, life might be like a box of chocolates, but it is more like a box of Tetris. Let me explain.

I have a good friend named Renee who runs an awesome company down in Louisville. She has a house in Florida and before she left to go down south, she gave Devin $5,000 to invest in growing the company and she gave Ryan $2,000 to invest in growing the company. She also gave Tim $1,000 to invest in growing the company.

Then she jumped on her flight to Florida and worked the whole time she was there, and hardly enjoyed the beach for a minute. I have no idea why she even left, but this is basically a true story.

So, how did Renee decide to give Devin more and Tim less? She looked at their abilities and gave accordingly.

Devin went out, traded with Chris, Brian, Nathan, Brittany, Travis, Chad, Matt, Ethan, and Anitza and ended up with $10,000.

Ryan went out and traded with Ashley, Chris, Ed, Mike, Christa, Lane, Cassidy, Sarah, Brandon, Scruggs, Corey, Tom, and Rishabh and ended up with $4,000.

Tim went out and put the money directly into his savings account. After a few weeks, Renee flew back to Louisville and asked Devin about the investment money. Devin said here's the five thousand you gave and here's five more thousand. Renee said, well done. Thanks for doing a good job with a little. Now I'm going to put you over two different departments.

Then Renee met with Ryan and asked about the investment money. Ryan said here's the two thousand you gave me, and here's two more from the interest we earned. Renee said well done... Now, we have this big opportunity to grow the business in a new market, and I'm putting you in charge of this initiative. Can you handle it? 10-4, said Ryan.

Then Renee met with Tim and asked about the investment money. Tim told Renee the good news. "I didn't lose any of it." Then he proceeded to hand her the full $1,000 back.

Renee replied... "Hmm, really? You weren't able to do anything to use what we gave you to try and generate even a little return for the company?"

Tim said, "Renee, I know you have high standards and you expect a lot from us, so I didn't want to lose what you gave me." Renee said, "I never care if you fail as long as you tried your best."

So, Renee took the $1,000 back from Tim and gave the extra money to Devin, knowing that Devin would invest it wisely.

That's a true story…

Hopefully you've heard it before.

A Stewardship Paradigm

That is and always has been one of my favorite messages, it is called the parable of the talents.[1] Of course, my version was slightly modified, but you get the picture.

Why should we love that parable? Because it doesn't matter what you were given. What matters is what you do with what you've received. This is called stewardship. You may have been given pocket aces and your peer was given less, but what matters is how you steward the gifts you've received. This is true in business and this is true in life.

The other reason that we should love this message is because it teaches us that we all have responsibilities. As Americans, we've been fed this unending malnutrition message of entitlements and privileges. Thus, Americans are generally starving for true meaning, responsibility, and a worthy reason to live.

Think about it this way... If you were to go out and earn a million dollars, wouldn't that satisfy you more than if someone were to just give you a million dollars? Anyone that will maximize influence in their sphere knows the correct answer.

THE PARABLE OF THE TALENTS SHOULD ACT AS A GREAT REMINDER THAT WE ARE NOT ENTITLED TO ANYTHING. INSTEAD OF FEELING ENTITLED, WE SHOULD TAKE REAL RESPONSIBILITY FOR STEWARDING THE GIFTS AND OPPORTUNITIES WE'VE BEEN GIVEN. KEEP IN MIND, TO WHOM MUCH IS GIVEN, MUCH IS EXPECTED.

And no, I don't pretend to understand why some people get cancer, or why my Dad died young, and why everything happens in life. And you shouldn't consume yourself with those things, either. If we fixate too much on why things happen, we'll forget to invest time to figure out what to do about it.

In one of the great TEDx Talks, Dr. Tasha Eurich discusses a study related to how widowers adjusted to life without their partners. The researchers found that those who tried to understand the meaning of their loss, were happier and less depressed one month later. But, if they were still trying to understand the meaning of their loss one year later, they were more depressed because they were fixated on what happened and why it happened, and forgot to move forward. In sum, self-analysis and introspection can be great tools to help stimulate growth, but too much introspection and self-analysis can lead us to immobility.[2]

At the end of the day, our focus should be on doing our best with the opportunities we've been given.

I DON'T DESERVE MORE AND I DON'T DESERVE LESS. NOBODY OWES ME ANYTHING.

This is how the world works, and this is also how the marketplace works.

The sooner we embrace this paradigm, the sooner we can start to live an undistracted life...

UNLEARN CONSUMPTION

"Over the last few decades we have been inundated by a torrent of words. Wherever we go we are surrounded by words: words softly whispered, loudly proclaimed, or angrily screamed; words spoken, recited or sung; words on records, in books, on walls, or in the sky; words in many sounds, many colors, or many forms; words to be heard, read, seen, or glanced at; words which flicker off and on, move slowly, dance, jump, or wiggle. Words, words, words! They form the floor of the walls, and the ceiling of our existence." – Henri Nouwen

We can easily agree that words are quickly subduing every crevasse of our lives. The quote above was written more than four decades ago (1981), before the internet became a commodity. Today, our computers, phones, tablets, video games, and TVs offer us more distractions than ever before. This oversaturation of words creates a reality that words begin to lose their meaning and we suddenly lose discernment of what is valuable...

IF WE ALLOW IT, OUR THOUGHTS WILL BE CORRUPTED WITH EMPTY IDEAS AND WORTHLESS OPINIONS, ALL OF WHICH ARE FIGHTING FOR OUR UNINTERRUPTED FOCUS AND ATTENTION. THEY ARE VYING FOR OUR TIME, ENERGY, BELIEF, AND RESPONSE... THEY ARE TRYING TO INFLUENCE US.

Let's look at the news for example. They use words to take the world's problems and try to turn them into your problems. That's how they make money, and it works. If it bleeds, it leads – and therefore *distracts*.

Are You Consuming or Creating?

When it comes to the news, are you consuming the news or creating the news? A life of influence is not about watching the headlines and then reacting accordingly, a life of influence is about creating. If there was one major difference between the influenced and the influencer, it would be this:

THE INFLUENCED ARE FOCUSED ON CONSUMING THE INFLUENCERS ARE FOCUSED ON CREATING

Please don't interpret the above phraseology incorrectly. True influencers are certainly consuming information and learning from other great influencers all the time. *The difference is, influencers don't consume to consume, we consume to create.*

Create for what?

- Create so we can help people
- Create so we can deliver insight
- Create so we can monetize ideas
- Create so we can give generously
- Create so we can change the world
- Create so we can hire more creators
- Create so we can inspire others to be their best

It is time to stop focusing on consumption and time to start focusing on creation… No more defense, it is time for offense. No more reaction, it is time to be proactive.

So, start to shift your mind away from consumption and focus on creation. Consumers pay, creators get paid. Your choice…

LEARN ADDITION BY SUBTRACTION

One of the crises we face today is not that we don't have good options to choose for consumption. We have plenty. The challenge today is that we have too many options, too many words, too many things to do, and too little discernment to help us choose and focus on the best option. How can we start to choose the best option? Well, it requires a fundamental understanding of some basic arithmetic.

Perhaps the most important math lesson I have learned over the years wasn't even in a math class. I was a freshman in college, playing soccer.

Our Coach at the University of Louisville was Ken Lolla, and he walked into the pre-practice board room one day and said: "Matt, Greg, and Bryan are no longer with us."

Zach (my closest buddy on the team) and I looked at each other and were pretty upset in the moment, especially about Bryan leaving us. He was one of our closest friends. He continued... *"Sometimes, we have to do addition by subtraction."*

And that was it, that was the whole conversation...

The very next sentence was something like this: We're going to start training today with Dynamic Stretching, 5v2s, Full Field 1v1s, and finish with 120 Yard Sprints until Chase pukes.

Alright, so I might be exaggerating that last part a bit, but that's pretty close to how I remember it. Ken was an excellent coach and those were very wise words, but at the time I didn't fully understand how important they would be to the rest of my life... Until Charlie Munger taught me the importance of throwing a viper down my shirt.

Let's take ourselves back to May 1, 2004. Somehow, we found our way to Berkshire Hathaway's Annual Meeting. The market was back on track and Warren and Charlie were the stars of the investing show. A lot has been written about Warren Buffet over the decades, but I'm amazed at how little media attention Charlie Munger gets in comparison. I've gone back and listened to these annual meetings over the years, but the 2004 meeting had some special soundbites.[3]

Audience Question: What are your thoughts on Compensation Consultants?

Warren: "We do not bring in compensation consultants... We don't have any human relations department, we don't have a legal department, we don't have a public relations department, we don't have an investor relations department. We don't have those things, because they make life way more complicated..."

Charlie: "I'd rather throw a viper down my shirtfront than hire a compensation consultant."

Just absolutely brilliant, that poor Charlie. But why do I share that with you?

It is not that Charlie hates compensation consultants, per se. He has simply trained himself to hate distractions. He has trained his mind to hate things that make his life more unnecessarily complicated.

In our world, we have words everywhere. We have worthless technology everywhere. We have distractions everywhere...

WE NEED TO START CHOOSING TO THROW VIPERS DOWN OUR SHIRTFRONTS BEFORE WE WASTE MORE OF OUR LIVES WITH THINGS THAT DON'T MATTER.

If you ever Pareto (80/20) your life, you'll probably find the same thing that almost all successful people end up finding... Most of the value or rewards we receive in life come from only a small amount of the actions we take. In other words, the majority of the output we produce comes from a small amount of the overall inputs. When we take time to consider it all, we'll find that we waste more energy doing things that don't matter than by doing things ineffectively, inefficiently, or even incompetently (we'll talk more about that later).

That's why I don't have any personal social media accounts. It's not that social media can't be a good tool for some, it's just not a great tool for me. It is also one of the reasons I haven't had a sip of alcohol in more than twelve years. I have a lot of priorities, and wasting my life scrolling through social media and drinking alcohol just aren't two of them.

We have a Maximize Value YouTube channel and a LinkedIn account, but I don't even know the passwords. I would literally have to call someone on our team and beg for the passwords to be able to access our accounts. It's not that these things can't be valuable. I'd simply rather throw a hungry viper down my shirt than waste more of my life majoring in the minors.

I made up this important song as a reminder for all of us. Let's sing it together:

GOOD IS THE ENEMY OF GREAT.
ELIMINATE. ELIMINATE.

Or just throw a viper down your shirt before you waste your life on stuff that distracts you from your dreams. And yes, vipers will surely help you stay focused, but then one day hopefully you'll wake up and realize you don't need vipers anymore.

That's the day you realize you learned how to get true freedom, which happens to be our next area of focus.

LEARN FREEDOM

There are few topics in the world that impact all of us, whether we are interested in them or not. Not a comprehensive list, but here are a few: health, relationships, culture, communication, time, and success. For now, we'll focus on the last item on the list.

Success is everywhere. It impacts all of us and confuses many of us. Everyone seems to think about it differently. When you ask people what they want in life, they often respond with some long-winded answer that finally ends up saying success. Then, if you care about the person, you ask them what success means to them. Most people will tell you that they want some sort of freedom.

Perhaps the most widespread agreement on the definition of success is this: I can do whatever I want, whenever I want, with whoever I want, for as long as I want. In other words, we feel like we have control of our time, or freedom to invest our lives however we choose.

Angus Campbell was a psychologist at the University of Michigan who researched what made people happy. Here is how he summed up his findings regarding his interpretation of the most powerful common denominator of happiness: Having a strong sense of controlling one's life is a more dependable predictor of positive feelings of wellbeing than any of the objective conditions of life we have considered.[4]

More than money, more than fame, more than a high IQ, more than a great body – having control to be able to do what you want is one of the main things in life that drives happiness. In other words, most people want freedom.

Which reminds me of my experience with baboons in Maputo, Mozambique during the summer of 2010.

Baboons & Freedom

On Friday mornings we would do some ministry at the bocaria (not sure of the proper spelling, but that is how it is pronounced), which was the most putrid and disgusting place on the planet, infused with some of the most wonderful people you'll ever meet.

After leaving the trash dump (it is a literal trash dump, not doing linguistic gymnastics) on Friday mornings, we had some time each week to explore the African bush, which was remarkable, by the way.

We had been there with the ministry team for a while when one of my missionary friends asked the guide how they find water to drink when they are thirsty?

Our guide explained how they set-up salt-traps for the baboons. Where we were in Mozambique, water was scarce but baboons were plentiful, and those in the bush know baboons love salt. So, what do the bush-folk do? They put a big lump of salt in a hole and wait for the baboon. The baboon comes, sticks his hand in the hole and grabs the salt. The salt makes the baboon's hand bigger, and the baboon's hand is now trapped in the hole. But the baboon loves salt so much that it won't let go of the salt. So, the men who live in the bush come and grab the baboon, throw it in a cage or tie it up to a tree and feed it a bunch of salt. What happens next? The baboon becomes thirsty and they release it knowing it will run directly to the water. The bush men follow the baboon to the stream, and voila...

Why do I tell that story?

Today, we are the baboons and the salt is cheap dopamine.

Baboons are addicted to salt. We are addicted to cheap dopamine. Addicted in the sense that we refuse to let go of the temporary pleasures even while knowing the addiction creates negative consequences.

There is an important lesson we should learn from the baboon, it is called:

FREEDOM FROM & FREEDOM TO...

IN ORDER TO GET
FREEDOM TO,
YOU MUST GET
FREEDOM FROM.

DON'T BE A BABOON.

Freedom To & Freedom From Examples:

[**Financial**] Freedom to buy whatever you want requires freedom from compulsively buying whatever you want.

[**Physical**] Freedom to enjoy a six-pack (abs) requires freedom from enjoying a six-pack (beer).

[**Psychological**] Freedom to enjoy peace of mind requires freedom from consuming anything stealing your peace of mind.

[**Relational**] Freedom to enjoy people who help you build a better life requires freedom from people who helped you build a bitter life.

[**Spiritual**] Freedom to worship God requires freedom from worshiping god(s).

[**Time**] Freedom to control your time allocation requires freedom from things controlling your time allocation.

EVERYONE WANTS FREEDOM TO. FEW WILL DO THE WORK REQUIRED TO GET FREEDOM FROM.

Will you do the work?

Once you do the work, you might find yourself with something valuable you could distribute to the world...

LEARN DISTRIBUTION

You have the power to change the world.

I'm not saying that to be trite. Every single one of you has one of the most powerful tools known to man...

An idea.

But, an idea is nearly powerless if it stays inside of you. That idea needs to spread, which reminds me of Ferraris. You know, Ferraris are safe in the garage, but that's not what they were made for. Ideas are safe in your head, but someone else could probably benefit from hearing your idea.

Everyone has an important story to tell, and I'd even take that to another level. I believe that God created you with a moral imperative to get your point of view, and your story out into the world. Everyone... Especially those who want to be real influencers.

But, most people don't have the courage or bravery to share their ideas. They are more focused on shielding themselves from criticism and judgment. After facilitating more than one thousand corporate training workshops, I have found that the fear of looking or sounding stupid is the main reason that more people don't share their ideas.

Please begin to ask yourself this question... Is it more important to shield myself from judgment than it is to take a risk and try to help someone? We all know the correct answer. But even still, sometimes that doesn't suffice.

So, if that doesn't work for me, I recite these truths to myself:

- Criticism says more about the criticizer than it does about you.
- People don't think about you nearly as often as you think they do.
- An honest person is as brave as a lion.
- He who jumps in the void owes no explanation to those watching.
- Your life will continue to improve when you remember that you can't and shouldn't try to please everyone.
- Truly successful people don't have time to criticize, we are all too busy working on our own meaningful work.
- Criticizing an artist is much more difficult to do when you have a paintbrush in your hand.

The Influence Equation

Why share? Well, your level of influence is a byproduct or a combination of two main deliverables:

1. Your Level of Expertise (Results, Insight)
2. Your Level of Reach (Visibility, Awareness)

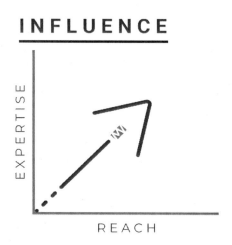

After a decade, or maybe less, I believe that most people develop some sort of expertise in their field. However, most people are obscure. In other words, nobody knows who we are or what we can offer the world.

If you have a story to tell (and you do) then just remember that the world will be slightly better because of you telling your story. Even if it only impacts one...

Corollaries on Distribution

First, always consider the cost of casting your pearls before swine.

Second, be ready to offend people when you share the truth. Whenever you share something controversial, you have to be willing to answer their questions. To me, this is not always worth the exhaustion. It is only because you are aware of how much these people drain your energy, and not for fear of their criticism, that it is wise to not always share your deeper insights in a large group setting.

The best formula I've found for solving this problem is to share non-controversial ideas with the masses, and have the deeper, more paradigm-shifting conversations in a small group or one-on-one setting. That said, always be ready to answer their questions with a few thought-provoking questions of your own.

Lastly, when you have an idea worth spreading... Share it. Use these tools to remind yourself that the full power of your idea can only be released when others benefit from it.

CHAPTER SUMMARY: PARADIGMS

Definition of Paradigm (emphasis added): A set of assumptions, concepts, values, and practices that constitutes *a way of viewing reality* for the community that shares them, especially in an intellectual discipline.

After delivering leadership workshops to thousands of people, I've realized that most people tend to focus a lot on behavior and very little on mindset. Both are certainly important, but I am convinced we have it backwards. Why? *Mindset drives behavior.*

With that in mind, there is nothing more important than knowing what we believe, and why. Our beliefs matter because they define how we perceive reality and they compel every action we take, every word we speak, and every decision we make. These paradigms or belief systems, are quite literally the way in which we see and interpret the world.

How much of our view of the world has been skewed by the powerful ideological mantras within our culture? In order to maximize influence, we must examine the extent to which we've allowed the modern onslaught of lunacy into every fiber of our being. No one else can do that for us, we must do it for ourselves. And yes, paradigms are complex things, but they are well worth thinking about if we want to help ourselves and others.

Within the context of influence paradigms, here is a summary of the six main topics in this chapter:

1. **Unlearn Narcissism:** Stop focusing on yourself and start focusing on helping others.

2. **Unlearn Entitlement:** Let's do our best with the opportunities we have received. Nobody owes us anything.

3. **Unlearn Consumption:** Our minds will be corrupted with worthless ideas if we don't learn to create instead of consume.

4. **Learn Addition by Subtraction:** Throw a viper down your shirt before you waste more of your life doing things that don't matter.

5. **Learn Freedom:** In order to have freedom to, you must get freedom from. Don't be a baboon.

6. **Learn Distribution:** The full power of your idea can only be realized when others benefit from it.

In the recipe of influence, nobody has a comprehensive list of all the necessary ingredients... But all of the topics in this book are a few of the non-negotiable ingredients within the recipe.

That said, we started the book with the main ingredient, which is paradigms. It is the main ingredient in our recipe because before we influence another person, we must learn to influence ourselves. In order to influence ourselves, we must understand our belief systems and the way we view reality. Onward...

CHAPTER 2

TIME

"He is no fool who gives what he cannot

keep to gain what he cannot lose."

– Jim Elliot

UNLEARN FIREFIGHTING

Look around you. What do you see? I see police officers chasing bad guys. I see call center reps addressing customer complaints. I see paramedics in ambulances reacting to car crashes. And most certainly, I see firefighters putting out fires.

I've seen so many people putting out fires that I've started to wonder if people actually enjoy the adrenaline rush of putting out fires all the time. Or maybe their dream was to be a firefighter but the local fire department wouldn't hire them, so they got a job in corporate America. I honestly don't know, but it has to be one of the two above options.

Perhaps this picture is best painted by a parable from Irving Zola, and it goes like this:

"You and a friend are having a picnic by the side of a river. Suddenly you hear a shout from the direction of the water—a child is drowning. Without thinking, you both dive in, grab the child, and swim to shore. Before you can recover, you hear another child cry for help. You and your friend jump back in the river to rescue her as well. Then another struggling child drifts into sight... and another... and another. The two of you can barely keep up. Suddenly, you see your friend wading out of the water, seeming to leave you alone. "Where are you going?" you demand. Your friend answers, "I'm going upstream to tackle the guy who's throwing all these kids in the water." [1]

You laugh now, but did you see yourself in that parable? You were the one going to save all those drowning kids. And what's more? You were frustrated with your friend who was going to tackle the guy throwing all the kids in the water. Have you ever been there? If your response is no, I don't believe you.

I guess we really love fighting fires and saving drowning babies. If we are honest though, it appears as if we are afraid to slow down and think about the future. Most of us cling to the adrenaline rush that leads us to saving as many drowning babies as we can, instead of pausing and dealing with issues that don't seem particularly urgent at this very moment.

Urgent & Important

In a 1954 speech to the Second Assembly of the World Council of Churches, former U.S. President Dwight Eisenhower gave language to the whole urgent task and important task conversation. Somewhere along the way, this concept was later turned into the Eisenhower Box (or Matrix). [2]

In 1989, this conversation was popularized by Stephen Covey in his famous book. He called it the Urgent Important Matrix.[3]

Many people give credit to Covey or Eisenhower for coming up with this interpretation of our time allocation, but if you really do your research on this, Charles Hummel deserves a lot of credit for giving us the deeper language and insight. If you are keeping score, this is what my scoreboard looks like. Eisenhower started the dialogue. Hummel expanded it. Covey made it popular.

In 1967, Hummel wrote an essay called the Tyranny of the Urgent and it is one of the most pragmatic concepts we've ever unearthed. So, what is the Tyranny of the Urgent? In essence, it is the constant tension that exists between the things we have deemed important, and the things we have deemed urgent on our daily to-do lists.[4]

He broke down everything we do into four quadrants:

>Quadrant 1: Important & Urgent
>Quadrant 2: Important & Not Urgent
>Quadrant 3: Not Important & Urgent
>Quadrant 4: Not Important & Not Urgent

For the sake of our time together, we will only talk about quadrant one and quadrant two. Why? Well, Hummel told us the other two quadrants weren't important, so I'll assume that your time is important and channel our energy to the two important items.

We all know plenty about quadrant one, but here are some examples of possible quadrant two activities: vision, mission, values, planning, coaching top performers, coaching for engagement, collaboration, process improvement, strategy, team-building, exercising, reading, praying, journaling, and enhancing relationships.

The Life Changing Power of Quadrant 2

Question for you...

What do you think would happen if we invested more time in quadrant two?

The answer may seem obvious to you. We would be forced to waste less time in quadrant one. Why? Because if we invest more time proactively solving problems, then we would have less problems to react to in the future. Think about it this way... If we tackle the guy who is planning to throw babies in the water before he throws the babies in the water, what happens? We don't have to waste our time and energy saving all the drowning babies. At the crux of the issue, when we invest more of our time with quadrant two activities, less of our lives will be wasted with quadrant one chaos.

Next question: What happens when we neglect quadrant two activities?

They eventually become quadrant one activities. How? Consider your health. Exercising is (usually) a quadrant two activity. If you go two decades without exercising, guess what will happen (unless you are a genetically gifted anomaly and a total freak-of-nature)? You will have some serious health issues you need to deal with. Most of these "should-do" things lie on a subtle, but very slippery slope and it is pretty easy to ignore your physical wellbeing for a while until you wake up one day in the hospital after having a massive heart attack.

TO MAKE THIS OBVIOUS FOR ALL OF US, QUADRANT TWO TASKS NEED TO BE OUR TOP PRIORITY BECAUSE IF WE PROACTIVELY DO THE THINGS WE SHOULD DO, THEN WE WON'T HAVE TO DEAL WITH ALL THE STRESS THAT COMES WITH LIVING A LIFE FULL OF CHAOS.

So, how do we do that?

The Psychological Priority Shift: Should to Must

An effective way to start being more proactive and less reactive is to fill your calendar with things you should do, and follow-through with them as if you must do them. Practically speaking, your daily agenda should be mostly full of quadrant two activities. Meaning, you prioritize the activities that will enhance your future and proactively prevent fires that don't yet exist.

In your brain, however, these quadrant two activities should be in the quadrant one category and you should refuse to go home until they are completed.

Example: I don't start my business day until I've invested at least fifteen minutes reading.

Technically, it is not that I "must" read every morning. I just know that if I don't do it before I start my workday, I know I'll never get to it. Then, all of the sudden, two years go by and I wake up spiritually inert and intellectually repressed. So, to proactively fix that problem before it becomes a real problem, reading has become a "must do" in my brain and on my daily calendar.

This psychological shift will help you, but please don't be naïve about it. We will still regularly have to put out fires, and you should block time on your calendar for "firefighting". Seriously, set aside time on your calendar that allows you to react and solve problems that seem urgent.

This is a lot like budgeting for new tires or an oil change. If you buy a set of 50,000 mile tires and don't plan to purchase new tires again until 100,000 miles… Shame on you. If you get an oil change that should last your car 5,000 miles but you try to drive 20,000 miles before getting another one, you can't blame someone else for the expensive vehicle repair bill. In the same context, we can't blame clowns for acting like clowns. We need to start blaming ourselves for going to the circus.

Thus, you must put new tires and oil changes within your financial budget and you must block time for firefighting on your calendar… Or what?

THE BILL FOR MISDIRECTING YOUR TIME ALWAYS COMES DUE

In the end, quadrant two is like the preventative medicine we need and quadrant one is the emergency surgery we have to endure because we didn't proactively take care of our health. How much longer will we keep putting ourselves through these emergency surgeries just because we won't eat a little healthier and exercise a little more? I don't know the answer, but I do know that if you want to be average, keep living in quadrant one. React, react, and react some more.

If you want to be a true influencer, start being proactive and start prioritizing the things you should do. Everyone accomplishes the things they must accomplish. It takes intentionality and purposeful focus to accomplish the things you should accomplish. It won't happen through osmosis.

Last question (from John Wooden): "If you don't have time to do it right, when will you have time to do it over?"

UNLEARN EXCUSES

Got it?

Yep, simple. Makes sense.

But...

I'm super busy right now, working on a major project for our department. Upcoming deadline for the client and it's currently all-hands-on deck. On top of that, my wife and I are renovating our house, and I am in the final stages of studying to earn my PMP certification. In about three months, this will all be over and I'm going to start waking up earlier, reading more, working out, eating healthier, going to church, saving for retirement, and then I'll even go back to school to finish my Master's degree.

Have you ever told yourself a story that sounds vaguely like that one? How long have you been telling yourself that story? Did the story ever come to pass? Is it time for a new story?

Maybe it is time to stop hoping for a time when you won't be busy. Why? There is a good chance that tomorrow is going to be just as crazy as today. If you wait for the perfect time to change, it will never happen.

Today is your day, now is the time. Start with one change today. Rinse and repeat tomorrow. Let this cycle run for about a month and then reach for the next. This is your new story. Out with the old story and in with the new. I'm optimistic that this will work for you.

That sounds great… But where do we begin?

UNLEARN DRIFTING

"Don't drift along taking everything for granted. Give yourselves regular checkups." – Paul of Tarsus

My beautiful daughters, Lael and Evie love to dress up and act like Mommy as they pretend to play the role of a Nurse Practitioner. Most of their doctor stuff is from the Doc McStuffins conglomerate and inevitably I get the privilege of being their most assessed patient. Before I receive my thorough assessments, we get to sing the following words… Cue the music.

Time for your checkup.

Time for your checkup...

You Are Here... Where Is Here?

Maps are fantastic. But, even the best maps are rendered useless if you don't know where you are... And most people don't.

That's why, in 2016, when we launched Maximize Value, one of the first things we built was a proprietary digital assessment platform. We realized the corporate training world was broken in several ways. First, the development world is filled with amateurs trying to teach professionals how to be professionals (this is why training can have a poor reputation). The second obviously broken thing was the methodology that most companies used to select content to deliver to their clients. So, we created an inventory taking tool that would involve everybody in the analysis process which would ultimately help us gather better data.

After all of the participants take the pre-training assessment, we respond with a pre-training proficiency report that analyzes the real growth opportunities from the mouths of those being developed. Then, we use the assessment data to drive the topic selection conversation. What is truly needed? Why did 95% of your team say they were terrible at coaching for accountability? Why did 75% say they were excellent at onboarding new team-members? This is important because it helps us take true inventory of the situation, and the same thing needs to happen with your time allocation. That is where the time log comes into play. It helps us understand where your time is going.

Are you drifting, or are you being intentional? I'll tell you where the average American wastes their time. Here's some data:

- The average American watches more than 4 hours of TV each day (A.C. Nielsen Co., 2019).
- The average US adult now spends upwards of 11 hours per day connected to linear and digital media across all devices and platforms (Nielsen's Total Audience Report, Q1 2018).
- Americans spend an average of 144 minutes on social media every single day (BLS, 2019).
- The average American spends 8.82 hours sleeping every day (BLS, 2018).
- The average American checks their phone 96 times per day (Asurion Research, 2019).

Those are all good data points. Provoking, I hope. But my favorite piece of data I have ever heard on this topic is that the average American wastes 55 minutes a day (roughly 12 days a year) looking for things they own but can't find (*Newsweek*). That one takes the cake for me.

Henry Ford put it this way: "It has been my observation that most people get ahead during the time that others waste." Truer words, never spoken.

Just look quickly at the statistics above. We literally just found at least 6 hours of time that most people waste every day (4 hours of TV + 1 hour of extra sleep + 1 hour looking for stuff). Think about that for a second. If that is true, then we waste an average of 25% of our lives on trash. That's just embarrassing.

You say, but Chase, I'm not the average American. And you're right, you are not. You know how I know that? Because the average American only reads one book per year, and if you are reading this book, it will probably not be the only book you read this year. So, let's say you waste only one hour every day… That's still too much, and we can do better.

How do we change this? The very first thing we must do is complete a thorough time log. I understand how excruciatingly boring this sounds, but I also know that:

IF WE DON'T TAKE TIME TO FIGURE OUT WHERE WE ARE, WE WON'T BE ABLE TO CREATE AN ACCURATE PLAN TO GET WHERE WE WANT TO BE.

How do we do this time log? Simply write down everything you do throughout the entire week with 15-minute block segments. The only item that you can group into a larger segment is your sleeping time. Everything else goes into a 15-minute segment. When it comes to the time log, the more detail you provide, the more helpful it will be. And yes, I am fully aware that you think this is common knowledge, but I can assure you that it is absolutely not common practice.

MOST PEOPLE WOULDN'T DARE TO LOOK AT WHERE THEIR TIME IS GOING BECAUSE THEY DON'T WANT TO TAKE THE RISK OF FINDING THE ANSWER.

They are ashamed at the potential of what they might uncover. Let's all remind ourselves that just because most people ignore the facts, doesn't mean they don't exist... Find the courage to take inventory first, then we can start to build a plan to live according to our priorities.

LEARN PRIORITIES

Tragedies happen every single day, all over the world. Some of them are completely random and seemingly unavoidable, while others are absolutely preventable. Both types of disasters are saddening, but the preventable ones are infuriating.

One of these avoidable tragedies happened on December 29, 1972 when Eastern Air Lines Flight 401 collided into the Florida Everglades, killing 101 passengers. That crash was one of the most horrific airline crashes in the history of the United States. So, what happened?

After an intense investigation, analyzing the components of the aircraft, the researchers discovered that all the vital functions and parts of the plane were in perfect working condition. Which led us to a deeper question...

What exactly went wrong?

The jet was preparing to land when the first officer noticed that the landing gear indicator light, was not lighting up. This particular little green light was designed to signal that the nose gear was locked down. Even though the light wasn't working properly, the nose was locked. In other words, the problem was the indicator light, not the actual gear function.

While the officers got distracted by the little light, they forgot to focus on landing the plane.

Here is an exact excerpt from the Aviation Safety Network:

> *"Probable Cause: The failure of the flight crew to monitor the*
> *flight instruments during the final 4 minutes of flight,*
> *and to detect an unexpected descent soon enough to prevent*
> *impact with the ground. Preoccupation with a malfunction of*
> *the nose landing gear position indicating system distracted*
> *the crew's attention from the instruments and allowed*
> *the descent to go unnoticed."* [5]

Long story short, the crew got distracted over something unimportant and 101 people died because of it. Which provokes me to ask the question: Are we like the distracted crew on Eastern Airlines Flight 401?

Maybe when we get distracted by silly things people don't lose their lives because of it.

Or do they?

TO WHAT YOU GIVE YOUR TIME DON'T YOU ALSO GIVE YOUR LIFE?

I wonder…

IF YOU LOSE A DAY OR YOU LOSE YOUR LIFE, ISN'T THERE ONLY A DIFFERENCE IN DEGREE?

Time is life, my friends.

This horrendous story leads us to the harsh realization that we often kill our time and ruin our own lives by doing things that don't matter. Which is a great reminder that:

THE MOST IMPORTANT THINGS IN LIFE SHOULD NEVER BE COMPROMISED BY THE LEAST IMPORTANT THINGS IN LIFE.

So, how can we get rid of the least important things in life?

How can we start focusing on the things that actually matter?

That's exactly where we are going next…

LEARN TO INVEST YOUR TIME

Time management isn't possible. There is only self-management.

No matter what we do, no matter how hard we try, we can't change time. It keeps going and moving whether we like it or not. But, we can and should manage ourselves more effectively, and doing that starts with using the Pareto Principle.

The most simplistic way to launch into better time investing is to learn to Pareto (80/20) your life. How do we do that? Three simple steps.

> **Step 1:** Write down a list of the top twenty things you invest or waste your time on in a given week.

> **Step 2:** Highlight the four that have the greatest impact on your results. Invest more time and energy with these four items.

> **Step 3:** Remove or minimize the other sixteen things.[6]

The Pareto Principle is brilliant, and it works. But, most people argue that they can't eliminate or get rid of tasks quite like business owners can, so they feel like they are handcuffed with this approach.

So, here's what we built at Maximize Value...

It is called the Maximize Time STAR Funnel and here's how it works:

1. **Remove or Minimize**

   Go through the list of tasks that are listed in your time log and ask yourself: Is there anything I can remove or minimize from this list? You may not be able to remove a whole lot, but you can probably minimize the duration of meetings or minimize the amount of time you waste sending emails.

2. **Automate**

   Then, ask yourself: What can be automated? For example, if you haven't set-up auto bill pay, you are losing time each month. If you haven't started to automate some of the regular email reminders you send, then you are wasting too much time each month. If social media is a part of your work and you aren't scheduling all of your posts to go out, then you are losing time each week. Let technology do some of the work for you (if you don't know where to start with this, contact me and I will connect you with my friend Stephen, a brilliant automation specialist).

3. **Transfer/Delegate/Outsource**

   The next question you ask is: What can I transfer to someone else? Who on your team could start to do that task for you? This is an opportunity to empower one of your team-members, but it also frees up your time in the long run. When you think about transferring tasks, always consider the following: Who is going to do what and when? Who is going to follow-up, and when? Who needs to be taught how to accomplish the what?

4. **Save**

And lastly, which of these tasks do I need to save time for in order to invest my time to create a better future? Start blocking time on your calendar for the important tasks that remain. In order to create a better future, you need to protect the time on your calendar for these particular items.

And yes, we get it. This is an upside-down way of thinking, and that's why we call it the Maximize Time "STAR" funnel. If you look at it upside down, the acronym spells STAR (Save, Transfer, Automate, Remove).

All of us can use the above methodology to start investing our time and stop wasting it. Why would that be beneficial?

Because time is life.

Life is short.

And every minute matters …

LEARN EVERY MINUTE MATTERS

If you want to learn how to be great at golf, study Tiger Woods. If you want to learn how to build wealth, study Dave Ramsey. He (and his team) have helped me and millions of people get out of debt and win financial freedom. He is a true expert. One of the first things he will recommend you do is to sit down with your spouse and create a budget. Simply put, a budget analyzes what is coming in (income) and what is going out (expenses or investments).

He created a tremendous budgeting tool for the world to use, and it is called *Every Dollar.*[7] I highly recommend Dave and this tool. But, we aren't talking about money right now, we are talking about time. So why would we bring up Dave Ramsey? Because the "Every Dollar" concept is absolutely brilliant, and it directly correlates to time. In essence, Dave tells you to give every dollar a name, and tell every dollar where it is going. In other words, there are no purposeless dollars in a good budget. The same goes for a time budget:

THERE ARE NO PURPOSELESS MINUTES IN A GOOD TIME BUDGET. EVERY MINUTE NEEDS A NAME AND SOMETHING IMPORTANT TO ACCOMPLISH.

The good news is, the "income" bracket in the time budget is the same every single day, no matter who you are or how much money you have. We have 1440 minutes that need a name.

There's a fantastic quote by author William Reilly that says:

"Everything requires time. Time is the only permanent and absolute ruler in the universe. But she is a scrupulously fair ruler. She treats every living person exactly alike every day. No matter how much of the world's goods you have managed to accumulate, you cannot successfully plead for a single moment more than the pauper receives without ever asking for it.

Time is the one great leveler. Everyone has the same amount to spend every day."

WHETHER WE ARE KINGS OR PAUPERS, WE MUST TELL EVERY MINUTE WHERE IT IS GOING. EACH MINUTE NEEDS A PURPOSE.

It is our responsibility to give it to them.

CHAPTER SUMMARY: TIME

You can have it all. You can have a family full of love. You can have a great spiritual life. You can help millions of people. You can earn an insane amount of money. You can have a great body. And you can have the freedom to do whatever you want. But you can't have it all right now. Why?

Because what you have today correlates directly to the decisions you made a decade ago.

But all we have is now. Tomorrow is never promised. Today, today, today...

The problem is not related to the current "be present" fixation. The problem lies in the short-term, instant gratification culture that exists today. And yes, I understand how difficult it is to develop long-term thinking when we live in a self-gratifying culture that preaches an instant injection could instantaneously deliver prophylaxis.

To achieve anything of significant value, there are no shortcuts. A physically healthy person is built over many years of consistent exercise, intentional nutritional intake, and living in a low-stress environment. Anyone selling physical or mental "wealth" via any other source is a charlatan.

If you are tired of taking advice from swindlers and trying these shortcuts that don't work, then start applying the fundamental techniques we covered in this chapter and watch what happens.

Here is a breakdown of the salient points we covered in this chapter:

1. **Unlearn Firefighting:** You won't have to save drowning babies if you move the "should-do" items into the "must-do" category.

2. **Unlearn Excuses:** Stop telling yourself that your chaotic life will slow down in a month. The best day to change is today!

3. **Unlearn Drifting:** Take inventory of where your time is going. Use the time log to help you get a clear picture of how to improve.

4. **Learn Priorities:** Don't crash the metaphorical plane because you are tinkering with something that doesn't matter.

5. **Learn to Invest Your Time:** Remove. Automate. Transfer. If there is anything remaining, save (block) time for what's left.

6. **Learn Every Minute Matters:** All 1440 minutes each day need a purpose, and something important to accomplish. Give it to them.

In the end, we can rest assured that the Spring will ask us what we were doing all Winter…

Will you be ready with the right answer?

CHAPTER 3

RELATIONSHIPS

"It is not good for man to be alone."

– God

UNLEARN DISTRACTIONS

September, 1997. Noblesville, Indiana.

The sun was shining brightly. The leaves were yellow, orange, and red. It wasn't hot outside, but it wasn't cold either.

I was wearing black, grass stained sweatpants with my Jerry Rice jersey and we were playing catch with a red, mini San Francisco 49ers football. Dad was the all-time quarterback (Steve Young impersonator), and of course we were playing in the Super Bowl against the Dallas Cowboys. When Dad threw a bad pass (rare), I do remember it was because Deion Sanders was blitzing and the pressure became overwhelming, so he had to throw it away.

In our back yard, we had about sixty yards with which we could play this made-up game called 4-Downs (thanks Uncle Curt and Flam). We had a

47

big soccer goal positioned at the edge of our property and the goal line for the soccer goal was dual purpose as it was able to manifest as an end-zone during football season.

The unwritten rule of this game is that you have four football downs to make it the length of the field to score a touchdown. That's the only rule.

After about an hour, I had successfully caught several diving touchdown passes to win the Super Bowl, so it was time to take a break and grab a drink. After a few minutes, I yelled: I'm ready to go, Dad. Are you?

Yep, just a minute, I want to tell you something...

"One day, you are going to grow up, get married, and have kids. Your kids are going to ask you to play with them. Your beautiful wife will ask for your time and attention. Your kids will ask you to watch them do a cartwheel, or watch them make a game winning three-pointer in the basement, or do a flip off of the diving board. Every time someone you love asks for your attention – you give it to them. You will always have excuses. There is always laundry to be done, dishes that need putting away, a yard to be mowed, or bills to be paid. Those things are far less important than your time with your family and loved ones. Stop whatever you are doing and give people your time and attention, you'll never regret it."

I don't remember what I said, but I do know that I was ready to go catch more touchdown passes.

Fast forward to August 17, 2012.

The worst day of my life, by far, was four days earlier. August 13, 2012.

On the 13th at approximately 7PM, the police showed up at that same house we were playing football catch. They found my Dad without a pulse on a running trail a few miles from our home and they asked my Mom to go identify him in the morgue.

On Friday the 17th, I stood before more than five-hundred people to lead my Dad's life-celebration service at our local church. Every seat in the house was taken, and there was no more standing room in the building. People had to stand outside to listen and pay their respect even though they came from all over the country to be there.

After the service, we had at least twenty people claim to be best-friends with Rexy. Probably more, but I don't want to exaggerate. Some of the aforementioned people we had never met or heard my Dad talk about before.

Story after story after story after story. There was a trend in how they all described my Dad.

"He was the best listener."

"He made you feel like you were the most important person on earth."

"He always dropped what he was doing to be there for you."

I guess when I was ten years old, those were just words keeping me from catching more touchdown passes. But to my Dad, those words were a maxim for how he lived his life.

Exemplum docet…

Latin for *the example teaches.*

Yet, today I am a teacher. I own a company that teaches people, and I've learned over the years that *what is taught is rarely caught.*

I can promise you on that autumn day in 1997, there were many things I didn't catch… But I caught the most important thing.

And you need to, too.

UNLEARN ISOLATION

In 1937, Dr. Arlie Bock and Dr. Clark Heath came together to try to start research on one of the most important pieces of data we've ever discovered. They wanted to start uncovering the common denominator between happy people and healthy people. What drives health and happiness? They asked.

Fast forward one year later to 1938, Dr. Bock and Dr. Heath went out and found this guy named John F. Kennedy, who was a sophomore at Harvard College. They asked him, and all of his peers in the sophomore class at Harvard to be a part of some research. They agreed. [1]

Then, they went out into the poorest neighborhoods in inner-city Boston, and asked some of the young men to be a part of this same study. In total, they started out with 724 young men.

What's most remarkable about all of this? The study is still going on today. It is called the Harvard Study of Adult Development and it may be the longest study of adult life that has ever been done.

When this all began, they had the young men complete physical examinations and the researchers even went into their homes and interviewed their parents. On top of that, they received complete medical histories from everyone involved in the study. The ongoing research is still pretty intense... Here's how it works:

- They interview them in their living rooms
- They get updated medical records from their doctors
- They draw their blood
- They scan their brains
- They talk to their children
- They video tape them talking to their wives about life

Every two years they completed questionnaires asking about their physical and mental health, marital quality, career or retirement enjoyment, and many other aspects of their lives. Every five years, health information was collected from the men and their physicians to assess their physical health.[2]

Almost all of the men from both groups have been interviewed every five to ten years to document more in-depth information about their relationships, their careers, and their adjustment to aging. Today, they've expanded the study and are now researching the 2,000 plus children of the original 724 men.

So, what came from the tens of thousands of pages of information that has been generated from studying these men? The clearest message that you can draw from the data is this:

GOOD RELATIONSHIPS KEEP US HAPPIER AND HEALTHIER.

Which leads me to believe that King Solomon was correct when he said:

BECOME WISE BY WALKING WITH THE WISE; HANG OUT WITH FOOLS AND WATCH YOUR LIFE FALL TO PIECES (THE MESSAGE).

Another major thing we can take from the research is that loneliness is one of the worst things for our health and happiness.[3] To quote Robert Waldinger, the fourth Director of the Harvard Study of Adult Development:

"LONELINESS KILLS. IT'S AS POWERFUL AS SMOKING OR ALCOHOLISM."

People who are more isolated from others find that they are less happy, their health declines earlier in life, their brain functioning declines sooner, and they live shorter than people who are not lonely. Isolation, in essence, has proven to be a literal killer.[4]

When they gathered all that they knew about the men at age eighty, they looked back to their data at age fifty. Cholesterol, blood pressure, and fitness levels weren't the best predictors of how healthy they would be in the future. The best predictor was how satisfied they were in their relationships. The people who were the most satisfied in their relationships at age fifty, were the healthiest at age eighty. [5]

You can read all about this data, but the best knowledge of this research can only be found in experiential learning...

My Experience

Suzanne, my beautiful bride, is from the Cincinnati area and is very close to her family. With us having kids, we always knew we wanted to be around family and in 2014 we ended up moving into the same neighborhood as my mother-in-law and father-in-law. To be exact, we live .24 miles away.

Jason, Erica (my brother-in-law and sister-in-law) and their little Naomi live .23 miles away from us and .01 miles from Janey and Jerry. Sam, Thomas, and their little Levi live less than ten minutes away and we are one big happy family.

Admittedly, I won the in-law lottery. Jerry and Janey are truly remarkable people. But even still, we all thought this close proximity might be a little much. And, as is often the case, I was way wrong. This is one of the best decisions we've ever made for our family.

Many people will argue that proximity isn't important and technology allows you to engage just the same. But these models are delegitimized by their outcomes. The internet certainly allows us to connect with people internationally, but the most meaningful connections require physical proximity. Why? Because we naturally help the people closest to us.

Maybe you are thinking that this approach doesn't work for everyone and maybe being that close to people you love sounds crazy to you. To me, it is crazy not to be close to the people you love. Life is too short.

I guess, in the end, what matters most about keeping healthy relationships is whether or not you are willing to put in the work...

UNLEARN RELATIONSHIPS ARE EASY

Have you ever heard of Pitocin? I hope not. It is nicknamed the pit, probably because some of its makeup has been derived from the pit of hell. I didn't know what is was either. And now I do.

My discovery of this drug happened in October of 2015. A few months earlier, Suzanne dominated her boards to be certified as a Family Nurse Practitioner. We were celebrating that milestone while simultaneously awaiting a much bigger milestone... Our firstborn child was scheduled to be born on September 22nd.

Waiting... and waiting... and waiting some more. 40 weeks, nothing happening. No contractions. No dilation. Fast forward to 41 weeks, still nothing. Fast forward to 41 weeks and five days – still nothing.

Finally, we made it to October 4th, 2015. At 6PM we arrived at St. Elizabeth hospital, not because Suzanne was having signs of birthing pains, but because they said we can't wait any longer, it is time to get this baby out and into the world. All signs were pointing to a healthy baby girl and a healthy Mommy. No problems there. The problem was that we just invested the last four months going through a natural birthing course and Suzanne was fully committed to enduring labor without any medication.

So what did she do? Well she changed her plans, of course...

Really?

No. Come on... Suzanne is a real-life superhero! Of course she kept the same plan. Action follows commitment... Didn't you know that already?

Important Note: All women who endure labor and bring a new life onto this planet are heroes. I'm simply telling a story about my stunning wife. Obviously, labor is a very complicated situation with nuances and variables that may require agility.

So, we arrived at the hospital and after a few hours of checking us in, they started with Cervadil right away. Contractions started shortly thereafter at 8PM. Then, at 10:35AM on October 5th, they started with the Pitocin.

For those that don't know what Pitocin is, basically it is pain in the form of an IV bag. That's all I could really gather from watching my beautiful wife in severe pain for hours and hours. In reality, Pitocin is supposed to amplify the frequency and intensity of your contractions. Ultimately "helping" you birth the baby.

At 12:30PM (still October 5th) Suzanne's cervix was only one centimeter dilated. This is not good news for those of you keeping score. On the notes that the nurse gave me (documenting the next 23 hours) all you see is this:

Pit on. Up dosage. Up dosage some more. Up dosage even more. No sleep. Two centimeters dilated.

There is something sobering or even maddening about watching the person you love most in severe pain.

Then at 11:14AM on October 6th, after 39 hours of labor pain... Our beautiful Lael was born. Finally. What felt like decades, also felt like mere seconds. It happened so slowly, and then so quickly.

Anyone who is a parent knows the purity of love you have for your newborn child. It's quite miraculous. But, there is nothing like the love you see when you watch a new Mother holding their first-born for the first time. Especially after 39 hours of intense pain, followed instantaneously by extreme euphoria.

After making time to think about and learn from the entire birthing experience, I came to a few conclusions... Maybe it is true? Maybe action really does follow commitment? Maybe Paul was right? Maybe love suffers long? Maybe true love endures all things?

I know this for sure...the purest love I've ever seen came after 39 hours of labor.

MAYBE THE BEST RELATIONSHIPS REQUIRE LABOR?

MAYBE ALL RELATIONSHIPS REQUIRE LABOR?

I've seen too many people I love get divorced. I've seen too many of my friends leave a great career because of a poor relationship with their boss. They were unwilling to put in the work. So unwilling that they decided to leave and start over instead of working through the pains of relational growth.

Starting over again can be repulsive. The path of less resistance usually requires you to just put in the work, which I know requires vulnerability...

LEARN VULNERABILITY

Vulnerability precedes trust.

The root word of vulnerability is vuln, which means wound. Simply stated, showing vulnerability can be interpreted as showing people your wounds. Not physical wounds, but emotional, psychological, and experiential wounds.

When the word vulnerability comes up, my brain automatically goes to when I was preparing for my first professional interview.

Question: Tell me about one of your weaknesses?

Don't you remember how they taught you to handle that question? Turn your weakness into a strength. I work too hard. I care too much. I am too detail oriented because I am a perfectionist. Blah. Blah. Blah.

Think about it. Just extending trust to someone requires you to be vulnerable. Owning a business teaches you this truth. When you first hire someone and you sign the front of their paycheck, and not the back of the paycheck, you learn that vulnerability comes before trust.

I was reminded of this when my friend, Mike Brown called me to ask for my advice. He said, "Chase, we are hiring over one hundred people and I need your help. What is the most important thing you look for when you hire someone at Maximize Value?" Great question, really made me think.

I ended up sending him these words from a poem written by Oriah Mountain Dreamer:

"It doesn't interest me how old you are. I want to know if you will risk looking like a fool for love, for your dream, for the adventure of being alive...

It doesn't interest me to know where you live or how much money you have. I want to know if you can get up after the night of grief and despair, weary and bruised to the bone and do what needs to be done to feed the children...

It doesn't interest me who you know or how you came to be here. I want to know if you will stand in the center of the fire with me and not shrink back."[6]

After reading that poem, Mike asked this follow up question:

"How can you know that they will be willing to do these things?

I didn't have a good answer in that moment, but now I do. In order for me to share the answer, I must share one of my favorite songs with you.

Here are a few of the lyrics from the song:

> *As a child, I had dreams of that future day.*
> *When I'd be the Pops I never had, glad the future came.*
> *You were my first, and you were my choice.*
> *And even though you're growing up you're still my baby boy.*
> *Adopted, into my name and you will carry it.*
> *A bond stronger than blood, my heart son you carry it.*
> *And where I've gone, I know that you'll go beyond.*
> *Your Daddy loves you Dom, I'm being real in this song.*
> *My son, I pray that you know, I pray ya know.*
> *That I will never ever let you go.*
> *And I will fight for you, and I will be right here. Right here.*
> *When you're tired and you're weak we can fight your fears.*
> *My son, I love you so.*
> *And your Daddy is so proud, thought that you should know.* [7]

You might read those words and think those are just words. Actions speak louder than words. Anyone can speak nice words into existence. And I agree, but hold tight and I'll address your shortsighted thought pattern.

Before you negate the power of those lyrics, please put yourself in Sean's (the artist's) shoes. First, think about how much raw vulnerability it took just to write that song. Then go and tell your son, that's how you feel. Then go and record that song and put it on an album. Then go and sell several thousand copies of that album. Then make that album available in most places that you can buy music.

Then consider the amount of people that could hear that song and might (incorrectly) say:

- Your music isn't very good
- Real men don't talk like that
- You're a pansy

If we truly can't recognize the amount of vulnerability that it took for Sean to produce that song, then we should probably invest some time to figure out how we developed such calloused hearts.

The Risk of Vulnerability

We can all agree that with vulnerability comes risk. There is a chance that some people will hold that raw genuineness against you in a negative way. But do we really want to be around those people anyway? I know I don't.

And yes, there are billions of people on this planet. Not everyone will like Sean, and certainly there are many that won't like Chase. And that's fine. We aren't for everyone. But the reality is, life is too short for all that surface level trash. This world is full of people that worship influencers who pretend to have an Instagram-perfect life. This prevailing societal problem has removed us from the depth of what builds authentic relationships. Let's go deeper. Let's go beyond the surface. Let's be real about who we are.

IF YOU ARE INSECURE ABOUT THE PERSON IN THE MIRROR, JUST REMEMBER THAT EVERYONE ELSE IS TOO. NOBODY HAS ALL THE ANSWERS, WE ARE ALL JUST LEARNING AS WE GO.

Back to the song.

The top reason that is one of my favorite songs is because of Tiger Woods. No, not really. The truth is, I love Tiger Woods and I'd love to talk about his greatness, but Tiger Woods is a fictional character in my brain. I've never met Tiger and I've never done life with him by my side. He is distant to me, and if I tell his story, I really don't know if it is true.

One of the reasons I love that song is because it provokes me to think of how great my Dad was, and it inspires me to want to be the best Dad for Micah (and my girls, too). But that's not the best part of the song. The best part about that song is the person who wrote it.

I can tell his story because I know the story is true. He is one of my closest friends on the planet, who also happens to be our Vice President at Maximize Value Consulting. I trust him with my life and with our company. Why? There are many things I don't know, but this I know for sure... Sean will stand in the center of the fire with me and not shrink back. It even says so in the song: *And I will fight for you, and I will be right here. Right here.*

Those lyrics were written for his son Dominic, but I know they carry over into our friendship, too.

That song came out in 2015. I started the process of hiring Sean in 2017. The vulnerability of that song was the predecessor to hiring him. When you hire a lot of people, you'll surely end up with some duds. But Sean's authentic, real, genuine vulnerability led to me hiring a friend that far exceeded my expectations and turned out to be one of the most trustworthy business partners you could ever find.

Back to Mike's follow-up question: "How can you know that they will be willing to do these things?"

The answer is, look for vulnerability…

ARE THEY COURAGEOUS ENOUGH TO BE AUTHENTIC? ARE THEY FEARLESS ENOUGH TO BE GENUINE? DO THEY PRETEND TO BE PERFECT OR DO THEY ACKNOWLEDGE THEIR OWN INSECURITIES?

Ask questions in such a way that will lead us to those answers. And maybe, just maybe…

One day your vulnerability will create genuine relationships that turn into deeply rooted engagement.

LEARN ENGAGEMENT

You might be saying, alright we get it. Relationships matter in life. I agree with you. But what about in our business? How do relationships show up on the bottom line?

To answer that question, I have to first talk about my hatred for the term work-life balance. I have a vitriol loathing for that term. Why? Because it implies that work and life are separate. It's just simply not true. It wasn't even true when it was just Adam roaming the Garden of Eden. After God made all the animals, He brought them to Adam and gave him work to do. His first job was to name all the animals. Work has been a part of our lives from the very beginning. The sooner we embrace that fact, the better off we'll be.

Now that we realize how work and life coincide, we can start to unpack how relationships drive profitability in the workplace.

Do you know how many people in the American workforce are engaged? Most data (including Maximize Value's) says less than 1/3 of the workforce is truly engaged in their work. For all of us math majors, that means about 2/3 of the workforce is either fully disengaged or partially disengaged.

Do you know what the number one driver of employee engagement is? Pay and Benefits. Just kidding, that's not even in the top three responses. Shame on you for falling for that one.

According to our Maximize Value Employee Engagement Research, by far and away, the number one driver of employee engagement is your relationship with your immediate manager. In other words, if the people who report to you say they are engaged in their work, they probably like you. If any of those same people are disengaged, you can do the math on that one. The good news is, you're the answer. The bad news is, you're also the potential problem.

Well, how does this correlate to profitability in our businesses?

Stop and think about it for a minute. What eventually happens if someone is disengaged?

They leave, right? What do we do next?

We have to replace them.

To understand the exorbitant costs associated with this, let's unpack the following questions:

- Were they a good producer when they were disengaged?
- Were they speaking positively about you and the organization when they hated coming to work?
- Did they steal time on the clock?
- Did they treat your customers and peers with excellence?
- How much did you pay to train that person?
- How do we find someone to replace them?
- Do you have a recruiter on staff?
- How much do you pay that person?

- How much money do you spend on sites to help you drive qualified candidates to your application page?
- How many interviews does it take until you offer someone a job?
- Who conducts the interviews?
- How much do you pay the people conducting the interviews?
- Once they start, how long do you need to train them? Who does the training? How much do you pay them?
- What kind of equipment and licenses do they need?
- What is the average time of "inactivity" for not having an employee in the seat of the person who just left?
- How much does that cost you?
- Do other people have to pick up the slack? Do you have to pay overtime? Is that a normal hourly rate or is it more?

I'm just getting started, the list goes on and on.

One of our partners at Maximize Value told us that it costs them $9,000+ just to get someone to start on their first day. That's how much goes into the recruiting and hiring process and that does not include any training or retention efforts.

There are several good research companies that calculate the cost of hiring, training, and retention. The best research comes from the company I own, because I trust the data more than all the others. We've found that it costs about the equivalent of 12 month's salary to replace an average performer, and it costs about 24 month's salary to replace a great performer. So, if they are making $50,000 and they are a great employee and they leave, then it will probably cost you about $100,000 to replace them.

We've also found that the number one variable cost in any company with more than 250 employees is turnover. Meaning, it shows up on the balance sheet in a significant way.

In fact, one of our partners said our Leadership Engagement Training helped save them $1.1 Million in retention alone, from 2018 to 2019.

Million. Have you ever touched a million dollars? I have. And it took a heck of a long time to be able to get there. And to see it all slip away because people leave your company? If relationships still don't matter to you, perhaps money does. So, what do we do about all this?

You go one step further than my Dad's recommendation. Instead of dropping what you are doing to be available for them, you instead block time on your calendar and plan consistent "Coaching for Engagement" meetings with all of your people. At a minimum, this should happen at least once every month. Here's what that conversation should look like:

COACH FOR ENGAGEMENT

1 BUILD AFFINITY	2 ENCOURAGE
4 IMPROVEMENT IDEAS	3 OFFER SUPPORT
5 VISION ALIGNMENT	6 EXECUTION ITEMS

THIS ISN'T COMPLEX OR SOPHISTICATED. IT IS EASY TO DO, BUT AS WE ALL KNOW, JUST AS EASY NOT TO DO.

Just remember that our world has changed and we don't live in an era where employees seek to demonstrate loyalty. Where they desire to start a career with one company, climb the ladder, and retire with the same company thirty years later. Today's marketplace is now impacted by intentional engagement more than ever before.

With that in mind please feel free to use our Coaching for Engagement process to drive performance and create overall buy-in (my copyright on this process is your right to copy).

If you've been using it for a while, you're probably winning loyal followers just like my friend Jeff...

LEARN LOYALTY

Take yourself back to 1998, a little before the anxiety that came with Y2K.

There was small building on Patty Lane in J-Town (Louisville). Today, I think they turned it into a laundromat. Back then, it was the birthplace of something great.

Daryl walks in for a short interview with some guy named Jeff. He walks out hired and ecstatic about making $10/hour without a college degree or much experience. Over the coming weeks Randy, Mike, Chad, and Gibbs all have a story similar to Daryl's.

The next week, they all show up to start their new drafting job. They won a contract to complete some drafting work for the Northern Kentucky region for their only client. Their drafting machines were ready to go, set up elegantly on folding tables in their little office. During the working hours, they traded files back and forth on 3.5-inch floppy disks and on break they traded hacky sacks back and forth until it was time to go back into the office.

Fast forward a few more years, to Daryl's 40th birthday. The team, Daryl's family, and several other friends were invited to celebrate Daryl's milestone birthday at Louisville Pizza Company. Jeff, the guy who conducted that interview many years ago, picked up the tab, and made sure everyone was there to enjoy the festivities.

Fast forward a few more years, and it is Chad's 20th anniversary with the company. Just like he threw Daryl a party, he threw Chad a $20K bonus check. That same bonus check is given to everyone else that hits the 20-year employment milestone with the company.

Yes, that's $20,000.00 extra dollars.

Years ago, I walked in to the local Ramada to deliver leadership training to 66 leaders. Daryl was one of them. I started by introducing myself to the group, followed by asking them how long they have been with the company? First person: 17 years. Second person: 17 years. Third person: 14 years. I didn't think much of it at the time.

1998, they had just a few employees. Fast forward to March 2020 and Rainbow Design Services has more than 500 employees. Of course, COVID happened and it forced them to go to a work at home model. I had a 1v1 with Daryl two days after the work at home mandate was announced. Daryl showed up to our meeting….

Chase: "How you doing my friend?"

Daryl: "I'm doing well, glad to be able to keep working with all that's going on right now."

Chase: "I hear ya. Has it been crazy for you?"

Daryl: "Yep, pretty busy, lots to do."

Daryl didn't tell me this, but I found out the next day that he was working about 21+ hours/day to get everything set-up for a remote workforce. He even slept in the office just so he didn't have to waste time driving back and forth. He and his team got everything ready to go in just a few days. Some sleepless nights in the office and about a million dollars later, Rainbow Design Services was equipped to handle the new work situation.

Chase: "Heard you slept in the office?"

Daryl: "Yep."

Chase: "Why would you do that?"

Daryl: "Do what?"

Chase: "Sleep in the office?"

Daryl: "I don't know. Didn't even think about it, really. It's just what was needed."

Chase: "That's pretty cool that you would do that. What is it about this place that keeps people like you so loyal?"

Daryl: "Hmmm. I don't know. I can't really speak for everyone, but I can say for most of us it's probably just the overall feeling of knowing Jeff took a chance on us, and we all really care about each other. I guess we just feel safe here. Maybe I could leave and go make more money elsewhere, but this place is like family to me. You don't leave family. Would you ever leave your family?"

In a weird, almost out of body type of experience as I was having this conversation with Daryl, I found myself feeling the exact same way. I felt a deep sense of loyalty to the Rainbow Design Family. At that moment, I remembered when I was about to start my entrepreneurial journey and I met with the Jeff, Renee, and Jason to tell them I was about to go and try to build a company and make this dream come alive. They probably don't even remember the conversation in the board room, but it changed my life.

Chase: I'm doing it. I'm going to give this entrepreneur thing a try.

Jeff: That's great, Chase. You'll do really well. You're an important part of our team... Please let me know how I can help you as you are getting started. Whatever you need.

I could tell you about a hundred stories of when I've seen or heard about Jeff demonstrating loyalty to me and other "family" members. A friend of a friend gets cancer and he goes out of his way to help. Toys for tots every year. Collecting food to give to people who need it. Leading fundraisers for important causes. Volunteering his time to support initiatives that will enhance the local community. Hiring friends of friends just to get them out of a hole and give them a chance at a better life. Giving people thirty chances to succeed. This list could go on for quite a while.

Loyalty is interesting, when you think about it. I'm not sure exactly how it works but I do know this:

YOU REALLY NEVER FORGET THE PEOPLE WHO BET ON YOU WHEN YOU WERE JUST GETTING STARTED.

Along those same lines, I have turned down a lot of money to deliver 1v1 Executive Coaching over the years. I don't know how much money I've turned down, but probably more than I would care to add up. We just don't offer that. It's not on our website, and from purely a financial standpoint, we lose money doing it. But I do 1v1s for Rainbow. Why?

WHEN IT COMES TO LOYALTY, YOU GET WHAT YOU GIVE.

CHAPTER SUMMARY: RELATIONSHIPS

If you really lived as if relationships mattered most to you – what kind of difference would it make in your family?

In your career?

In your life?

When we use these relational best-practices consistently, we will uncover the greatest win in life – which is helping others grow, succeed, and tap into their potential. Your application of this chapter can help you have a part in making that happen for the people in your sphere.

Here is a breakdown of the salient points we covered in this chapter:

1. **Unlearn Distractions:** Laundry, dishes, bills... Those things are far less important than time with your loved ones.

2. **Unlearn Isolation:** Being alone is a killer, but great relationships keep us happier and healthier.

3. **Unlearn Relationships Are Easy:** Love suffers long and all relationships require labor, so be willing to put in the work.

4. **Learn Vulnerability:** Find people that are courageous enough to be authentic and fearless enough to be genuine.

5. **Learn Engagement:** Engagement builds relationships and drives profitability. Block time to create connections with your people.

6. **Learn Loyalty:** When it comes to loyal relationships, you get what you give.

CHAPTER 4

COMMUNICATION

"The bill for miscommunication always comes due."

— James Clear

UNLEARN SOCIOTROPY

Have you ever been to a Holocaust museum? If you haven't, have you ever wondered how something so horrifying could ever happen?

In December of 2014, before Lael was born, Suzanne and I traveled to Israel for a few weeks. It was absolutely stunning. One of the days, we invested several hours touring Yad Vashem, which is Jerusalem's Holocaust Museum. This was certainly one of the most marking moments of our Israel experience. We were only there for less than half a day, but I'll never forget it.

When you walk inside the museum you'll see a huge cart full of shoes from victims of some of the concentration camps. This paints quite a picture.

After the shoes exhibit, you'll get to experience what they call The Hall of Names, which is a memorial to each and every Jewish person who died in the Holocaust. This is eye-opening, to say the least.

But, the part of the museum that was most thought-provoking for me was the Children's Memorial. This is an underground cave, mostly dark, but you see small flames of light representing the approximately 1.5 million children who were murdered during the Holocaust. The most penetrating part for me was hearing the recorded voices call out the names and ages of these blameless, beautiful souls.[1]

After leaving the place, you might ask yourself a couple questions. First, how could anyone ever allow this to happen to another human being? Secondly, how could so many people stand there and allow this to happen to these innocent kids who could not protect themselves?

We were in Israel with our friends Cy and Jill and we were debriefing our adventure for that day. Jill asked: "How could so many people be guards at Auschwitz and live with themselves?" This is a question I've revisited and re-read from my journal many times since that day.

How do you get to a place where you allow these things to happen right before your eyes? Is it a slow and slippery slope?

Do you wake up one day and just decide to be nihilistic?

I'm not certain, but here's what I do know for sure...

Influence & Sociotropy

After experiencing and watching what our world went through in 2020, I am starting to realize why so many people allow bad things to happen right before their eyes. It is a personality trait called sociotropy. [2]

Important Note: Before we talk about sociotropy, please know that our world today and the world that existed during the Holocaust are extremely nuanced, and this explanation isn't even close to comprehensive. I've simply found this to be one of the major contributing factors as to why many people don't communicate the truth.

What is sociotropy and why does it matter? In sum, it is the more formal or more clinical terminology for people pleasing. There is more to it than my explanation presents, but in its most basic of definitions, this suffices.

Not only do people with sociotropy want to please people, but they tend to fear the disapproval of others and avoid conflict like the plague. These people don't want to make any trouble, and having someone mad at them can be downright terrifying. In short, their approach to relationships goes beyond being kind and helpful to being crippled by fears of interpersonal conflict. They tend to try desperately to keep everyone happy. Creating tension is sinful and social acceptance is paramount.

How does this connect to influence? Well, sociotropy is almost always linked to a lack of assertion. Individuals who are sociotropic generally avoid confrontation to prevent discomfort and they have higher levels of anxiety with situations that involve any possible tension.[3]

So how do we overcome this sociotropy thing? First things first, we need to understand that intentional growth doesn't happen within our comfort zones. There is no growth within your comfort zone. Tattoo that on your brain if you haven't already. And always remember...

IN ORDER TO HELP PEOPLE GROW, YOU NEED TO BE WILLING TO GET OUTSIDE OF YOUR COMFORT ZONE... AND HELP OTHERS DO THE SAME. ALSO, CONSIDER THAT THE LEVEL OF COURAGE YOU HAVE WILL, IN SOME WAYS, DIRECTLY CORRELATE TO THE NUMBER OF UNCOMFORTABLE CONVERSATIONS YOU ARE WILLING TO HAVE. BOTH WITH YOURSELF, AND WITH OTHERS.

With that in mind, we need to remind ourselves that when we have to coach people in truth, it is not being conducted because we did something wrong. We didn't show up late. We didn't speak inappropriately. We didn't have the bad attitude. We weren't scrolling social media during work hours. We didn't miss work and not properly inform our manager. They did. Actions have consequences. That is not a mean thing to say... We can say that if we truly love people enough to tell them the truth. The truth will set them free.

Many of us try to blame ourselves for the gap that exists, and it is important to remember that they were the ones that chose not to meet the standards that were set forth by the team. It is not your fault that this difficult conversation is taking place. They missed the mark, and it is your responsibility to address the issue. The size of your paycheck depends on it.

Corollary: Before addressing a gap, always look in the mirror first. Were the expectations explicitly clear? If not, have a difficult conversation with the person in the mirror. If the expectations were clear (and you have evidence of this) then you need to go address this gap with the truth.

In the end, we need to remind ourselves that we will pay the price either way. There is a price for saying the truth. There is a price for not saying the truth.

Which price do we want to pay?

We can stand there and pretend nothing happened, but the price for doing that will be evident when our people take an inch and turn it into a mile. When we don't address these gaps, we are propagating the message that this behavior is acceptable. We aren't saying this is acceptable behavior, but when there is no consequence, that is how they interpret the situation. Perhaps there is a deeper metaphor within this paragraph.

Count the Cost

In 2019, I delivered over 200 workshops. If we do the math, that's more than 36,000 minutes of having the privilege of sharing a message with an audience.

When you have the honor of speaking for a living, and you get to do it before thousands of people and for more than 600 hours in a year, you start realize that you will eventually offend people. I realized this truth, and I began to count the cost of the role that I get to play in these different organizations.

There are many days when I am faced with the choice of sharing the truth or being silent, and I am disappointed to say that I've done both. But only one of them kept me up at night. If you are influencers for long enough, you will have the same opportunity. Do I address the gap? Or do I let it go and pretend it never happened? Do I share the truth, or do I turn my back on my values?

When we realize this fact, we recognize the need for speaking the truth. And let me tell ya, be ready to offend people if you value the truth. This doesn't mean that we will always offend people, it just means that we need to be ready to offend people. Sometimes the truth can sting.

Note: Some people love to interpret this message as if they need to hold people accountable in an aggressive way or a harsh way. This is wrong. Do it, but do it with tact. You can be kind and assertive at the same time.

We will always have to live with the consequences and we will always have to pay a price.

And because this can't possibly be over-considered, I am asking this question one more time: Which price do we want to pay?

It is not safe to share the truth, and it never will be.

And as I learned at Yad Vashem, it is even more damaging to just stand there and watch.

UNLEARN TALKING

In 1962, Al (A.R.) Sullivan and his Dad (A.O. Sullivan) took a risk and founded Sullivan University, which expanded into the Sullivan University System. They grew it into several campuses, more than 1,000 employees, and many millions in revenue.

Exactly fifty years later, 2012, a young twenty-nothing whipper-snapper walked over to Al Sullivan's office and asked him if he could take him to lunch.

Chase: "I'd really like to pick your brain about entrepreneurship and hear the story about how you and your dad built this business. Can I take you to lunch?"

Al: "Sure, that would be great. How about next Friday. Winston's?"

Chase: "Perfect. I'll see you there."

Dressed in an oversized navy suit, I sat down in Al's favorite spot in the corner of Winston's (he owns Winston's, by the way). A little nervous, but mostly excited about being able to learn from Al, I came prepared with a notebook full of questions to ask. When Al showed up, we shook hands, sat down, and he took control of the conversation right away.

Al: "This morning I was reading over your resumé and it looks like you spent some time serving at an orphanage in Africa. Tell me about your experience over there."

Al: "Jim told me that you and Jimmy Crick are really close friends and you built your friendship while playing soccer at Louisville. What was it like being on one of the best teams in the country?"

Al: "I really like your coach, Ken Lolla. What was it like playing for him?"

Al: "You've done a great job with stepping in and making a difference right away. In what ways can we make this an even better place to work?"

Question after question after question. I walked away from our lunch meeting with several notes, yet I only asked him one question from my list of twenty-plus questions. Al Sullivan is a brilliant business mind, one that I had the privilege of learning from. Some of the learning came from up-close, the rest from afar. That said, I am not really sure what Al took away from our lunch meeting, but I took away a lot. One of the most important things I took away from that meeting was how much I liked Al as a person, and therefore how much I believed in working for the Sullivan family. It was a great place to work, and my favorite place to work, except for Maximize Value (of course).

The other mind-blowing thing I took away was the fact that he spent time reading through my resumé. When he said that, I'm sure my jaw hit the floor. Do you know who you are? That is probably the question I was asking with my facial expressions. You took time to read my resumé and do research about me? That lesson reminded me that it doesn't matter how successful you are or how successful you think you are, people mostly only care about you when you care about them. Which reminds me of this truth:

EVERYONE SEEKS TO BE UNDERSTOOD.
FEW SEEK TO UNDERSTAND.

With that in mind, in 2018 our Maximize Value team conducted a research study that lasted over a year. We asked hundreds of people one question:

WHAT MAKES A GREAT LEADER?

The most common response we received in our research:

MY LEADER CARES
ABOUT ME AS A PERSON

When you are looking for a place to work, find a way to get around people like Al Sullivan. People that care enough about you to ask you about your story and listen to your answer. Which reminds me that the best listeners are not the most silent. The best listeners are the ones who ask the best questions. The best questions help us understand people more comprehensively and they help us uncover ways we can help people on a more individualized level. How does this help us as influencers?

A GOOD WAY TO END UP
GETTING WHAT YOU WANT
IS TO HELP OTHERS GET
WHAT THEY WANT.

How do we find out what they want?

UNLEARN MOTIVES

On Saturday mornings in the Summer, Mike and I always grab the 6:30AM tee time. Our goal is to walk nine holes early in the morning and be home before our wives and kids are ready to start the day.

One Saturday morning after golf, Mike said... "I need to stop at Home Depot really quick and buy a ¼ inch drill-bit."

Chase: "Why do you need a drill-bit?"

Mike: "Brittany was out last night and bought some new art picture that she wants me to hang in the living room. I have the anchors and the drill, I just need the bit."

Which leads me to this question... Have you ever purchased a drill-bit? My guess is, like Mike, that you didn't purchase the drill-bit because you wanted the drill-bit.

How do I know that, because nobody in the history of mankind has ever purchased a drill-bit because they wanted a drill-bit. When you purchased the ¼ inch drill-bit, you probably wanted a ¼ inch hole in your wall. But does anyone honestly want a hole in their house? The answer is no. Then why buy a drill-bit? Well in Mike's case, it was to hang some art in the living room. But did Mike care about the art? No, actually probably the opposite. He probably didn't want anything to do with the art. So why did he go and buy a drill-bit that he didn't want, drill a hole in his house that he didn't want, and hang some art that he didn't want?

Despite his major shortcoming of being a UK Wildcats fan, Mike is actually a really smart guy. You see, he knows that a happy wife usually leads to a happy life, and he wanted to make Brittany happy by hanging her new picture for her. But is that all Mike wanted? No. We all have selfish motives. All of us.

You see, Mike and I play in a basketball league on Sunday nights and he knew that if he was going to play golf with me on Saturday morning and be able to play in our basketball game without feeling guilty, he needed to get his honey-do-list completed before game-time.

Did he want a drill-bit? No. Did he want a hole in his house? No. Did he want to spend money on art? No. Did he want to hang it in his living room? No. Did he want a happy wife? Yes. Did he want the freedom to be able to enjoy his Sunday evening playing basketball with the guys? Yes.

So, what's the point?

WHEN WE ARE TRYING TO SELL A NEW IDEA OR A NEW PROCESS, REMEMBER THAT NOBODY CARES ABOUT YOUR IDEA OR PROCESS. THEY ONLY CARE ABOUT WHAT THE NEW IDEA OR NEW PROCESS WILL DO FOR THEM. HOW WILL IT MAKE THEIR LIVES BETTER AND EASIER?

If your job is to sell drill-bits for a living, you'll have skinny kids if you talk in terms of drill-bits. When you start to tailor your language to the individualized motives of the target audience, your kids won't be as malnourished. Start talking in terms of happy wives, and freedom to watch the game or hang with the boys when they have their honey-do lists completed.

This idea can't possibly be overstated. People don't buy you, they buy what you do for them. They don't like your idea, they like your idea because of what it does for them. It is only when you start to talk in terms of what matters to them that your winning percentage will increase. It is your job to communicate in a way that makes them the hero.

Speaking of heroes...

LEARN THE HERO STORY

How can I become a better communicator? Learn the art of storytelling. Why? Stories help people remember what matters. Facts, data, and numbers can be excruciatingly boring, but people tend to remember good stories.

Stories are fundamental to how we connect as humans. If you deliver the story with tact and precision, you may inspire, persuade, entertain, and teach – all in just a few moments. According to research by Vanessa Van Edwards, the quickest way to get someone on the same page as you is to tell them a story.[4] I agree.

And we all agree that a good story unfolds when we see the salient points come alive in the verbiage. When the storyteller provides context, details, and proper framing – we can start to paint a picture of the who, what, when, where, how, and why. So how do we frame these stories to captivate our audience?

In the story of how you influence the world, you need to begin to construct your framework around the true heroes in your narrative. There are thousands of ways to format our stories, but I've found this approach to be useful.

Start by identifying these five key puzzle pieces:

1. **A Hero:**

   The hero is never you or your business. It is always the person you help (your customer). The hero is the one transformed as the story progresses.

2. **Your Hero's Current Reality:**

   Identify where the hero is today and why they are there. This is the starting point of the story.

3. **Your Hero's Desired Reality:**

   Where does the hero need to be? Why? What will he/she be able to do with your help that he/she can't do now?

4. **A Barrier:**

   If the transformation was easy, the hero would not need your help. What is keeping the hero from their desired reality?

5. **A Helper:**

   If the customer is the hero, how do you come into play? If your customer is Michael Jordan, you are Phil Jackson. You have helped the hero by giving them the tools that allow the hero to achieve the desired reality. To better understand how you come into play, think about what problems you solve. To what questions are you the answer?

And of course, most good stories end with some sort of take-away. In other words, what is the moral of the story? Sometimes the most sophisticated stories leave it to the audience to figure out the moral of the story. Sometimes the take-away is spelled out with clarity, which is where we need to go next.

[Note: There are several examples of the hero story in this book. You can find one in the chapter on Serving. Ryan is the hero, my Aunt Susan is the helper. You can figure out the rest.]

LEARN CLARITY

Uncertainty is the driver of most stress.

While most of us know that uncertainty and ambiguity are catalysts for producing cortisol, why do we lack clarity so often in our communication?

My favorite study that paints this picture is from Elizabeth Newton, a Ph.D in Psychology from Stanford.[5]

For her dissertation, she created this simple game in which she assigned the participants into one of two groups:

Group 1: Tappers
Group 2: Listeners

The tappers received a list of twenty-five well-known songs like *Happy Birthday to You* or *The Star-Spangled Banner*. The tapper's job was to select a song from the list and then tap out the rhythm (by knocking on a table) of the song for the listener to hear. The listener's job was to decipher the tapping and guess the song.

After one-hundred and twenty attempts, the listeners were only able to guess the correct song three times. That means 97.5% were incorrect.

But here's my favorite part. Before the listeners guessed the name of the song, Newton asked the tappers to guess if they thought the listener would provide the correct answer. 60/120 of the tappers thought the listener would guess correctly. For all of us math majors, that's 50%.

What does this mean? It means there was a 47.5% gap in clarity.

How is this possible? I see this experiment reenacted every day in the marketplace between the C-Suite and the frontline associates. We often assume that everyone else knows what we know and it is time to change our assumptions. We can start to enhance our communication clarity with one simple daily approach. We, at Maximize Value, call it Say – Do – Say...

Say:

This is the first phase, which is saying what you will do. This may include a statement of work or a simple email where you outline what will be accomplished. Remember: Who, is going to do what, and when? Make sure all of that is included in this first phase of project communication.

Do:

In this step, you simply deliver on what you said you were going to do. This is the easiest step in the process if you did a good job of setting yourself up for success (clear scope of work). Just remember, do what you said you would do.

Say:

This is the "Eureka" moment for many of us. In this third step, we simply say what we did in the "do" portion of the process. This may come in the form of meeting minutes or a simple recap email to all necessary stakeholders. Just remember, who did what, and when. What were the salient points from the meeting or the event. What are the next steps?

REMEMBER, TO BE UNCLEAR IS TO BE UNKIND.

CLARITY IS KINDNESS.

LEARN SELF-DISCOVERY

Have you ever been to an awards ceremony that turned into not an awards ceremony really quickly?

I've been there. I was meeting with Brian Willett at the local Panera, just a few miles from our home. We were meeting to go through my formal annual review. Before our meeting, he sent me a version of the review to evaluate myself, and then he told me he would be filling out the same thing for me. I quickly completed the document by giving myself high scores in almost every area and sent it back to Brian. He filled out the same evaluation for me and really gave it a lot of thought.

Our meeting started off very positive, with lots of rapport and encouragement. Then we got to the review, which also started off great... Until we got to the non-award-ceremony part of the dialogue.

Here's how I remember the conversation:

Brian: I want to help you. I'm not here to criticize you. You add a lot of value to our company. The easy thing would be for me to just not even have this conversation with you. I could just say you're great and we could both go on and live happy lives. But, I care too much about you to not share some feedback with you. I could easily give you really high scores and send it in and it would be fine. But that doesn't help you improve.

Chase: OK...

Brian: What happened when you interviewed that one guy that ended up not taking the job we offered him?

Chase: I'm not sure what you are talking about.

Brian: Do you know what he said?

Chase: No idea.

Brian: He said he didn't want to work with you.

Chase: OK.

Brian: Don't you want to know why?

Chase: We already hired someone for that position, let's move on. Do we really have time to sit around and wonder why he didn't take the job?

Brian: Don't you think, as our Cincinnati Leader, that it should matter to you? Isn't part of your role being able to attract top talent to our team?

Chase: If he doesn't want the job, I'm not going to hold his hand and make him want a paycheck from us. Should we really waste our lives worrying about this?

Brian: No, I'm not wasting my life worrying about this. I'm worried that if I don't share this feedback with you, you won't ever achieve your full potential. Doesn't that matter to you?

Chase: Yes, definitely.

Brian: We all come across the wrong way sometimes, and sometimes we don't even recognize it. I know how great you are, and I want other people to experience your greatness, too. This isn't about you being in trouble... I just invested the last hour talking about how many good things you do. This is about you becoming the best version of you. I care about you enough to have this conversation with you. All that I ask is for you to start to think about your interactions with people and start to think about what you can do differently to make sure they experience you in a more positive way. The way that I experience you.

Chase: Thanks. I'll think about it...

After thinking about it, I finally realized how foolish I was acting...

"THE WAY OF A FOOL IS RIGHT IN HIS OWN EYES, BUT HE WHO HEEDS COUNSEL IS WISE." – KING SOLOMON

It took a while for me to understand the value of that conversation with Brian. It wasn't until weeks later that I actually allowed myself to process the dialogue and discover where I was missing the mark. I wrote about that interaction in my journal, and I've thought a lot about that back-and-forth since that day, and I've changed for the better because of it.

It wasn't until years later that I thanked Brian for being willing to have that conversation with me. He really didn't need to do that, but he valued our friendship enough to ask some of those hard questions that really made me think. We all need people in our lives that will ask us the hard questions that will eventually yield self-discovery. Some of the most important moments of my life came from people who were willing to challenge me and have a thought-provoking conversation with me. They knew I needed to open my eyes to more self-awareness.

(Note: to become more self-aware, we need to start by recognizing that we aren't as self-aware as we think we are.)

In that particular situation, Brian didn't yell at me and tell me to change. He asked questions to help open my eyes to my behavior gaps, which is a much more effective way to help lead people to behavior change.

The Value of Self-Discovery

The most effective coaching processes and sales processes are centered around asking questions to produce self-discovery. The best influencers will intentionally ask questions so you can take inventory of where you are and why you are there. It would be much easier for us to create a game-plan for you and tell you what to do, how to do it, and when to do it. This methodology has proven ineffective.

THE BEST INFLUENCERS DON'T TEACH YOU WHAT TO THINK, THEY TEACH YOU HOW TO THINK

In order to influence people at the highest level, we must create an environment of self-discovery. We ask challenging questions, and in return, you tell us what you need to do to be the best version of you, rather than us telling you how to become that person. The self-discovery methodology is valuable because of the buy-in it creates. When you come up with the idea, the likelihood of you following-through to execution and habit formation increases exponentially.

Because of that conversation with Brian, I self-discovered where I fell in this particular chart:

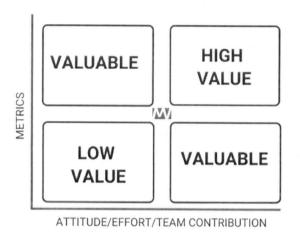

Metrics: Great

Attitudes: Some Great, Some Not Great

Effort: Great

Team Contribution: Not Great

If Brian didn't have the courage to have that conversation with me on that day, there is a chance I would have gone through my leadership life without understanding that my paycheck is a reflection of how much I contribute to the overall team. Not just in metrics, but in synergy, camaraderie, and chemistry. Not just with my direct-reports, but with my peers.

Perhaps the greatest metric we could use to identify the impact this conversation had on me is the quality of my friendship with Brian today. Several years later, he is one of my closest friends. I guess iron really does sharpen iron... Which reminds me of this quote from Tom Landry:

"A coach is someone who tells you what you don't want to hear, who has you see what you don't want to see, so you can be who you have always known you could be."

At the end of the day, we all need to be a little more like Brian. Care enough about your people to ask them the hard questions so they can self-discover.

CHAPTER SUMMARY: COMMUNICATION

Communication, from the Latin word *communis*, meaning common. Effective communication requires the establishment of commonality. More commonality equals more connection and greater communication.

To communicate more effectively, let's apply the six core concepts we covered in this chapter:

1. **Unlearn Sociotropy:** The desire to please people is dangerous because it leads us to not sharing the truth.

2. **Unlearn Talking:** Stop talking and start listening. The best listeners ask the best questions.

3. **Unlearn Motives:** Nobody cares about your drill-bit. They care about what the drill-bit does for them. Tailor accordingly.

4. **Learn the Hero Story:** Stories help people remember what matters and they are fundamental to how we connect as humans.

5. **Learn Clarity:** To be unclear is to be unkind. Use the Say-Do-Say approach to stop the misinterpretation.

6. **Learn Self-Discovery:** The best influencers don't tell their people what to do, they ask questions to create self-discovery.

CHAPTER 5

CULTURE

"People support a world they helped create."

– Dale Carnegie

UNLEARN METRICS

If you want to know how to write a great book, go to James Clear. If you want to learn how to be a great basketball coach, go to Chris Mack. If you want to know how to build a great culture, you need to go directly to my guy Chris Reese.

Walk into Chris Reese's Arizona office and you will notice a lot of personal items and family pictures. Then you'll see some Phillies Gear and Eagles memorabilia, paying homage to his beloved Philadelphia hometown. Aside from the Philly décor, the next thing you'll notice in Chris's office is a yellow poster hanging at eye level with several reasons listed about why employee engagement matters.

Then, perhaps the most noticeable item in his office is the big wooden block on the wall, which was split right down the middle with an axe.

He took the team out for a synergy event at Lumberjaxes Axe Throwing and one of his managers, Jason, hit the bullseye. Chris took the woodblock back to the office and displayed it as a memory from the camaraderie experience.

Leave Chris's office and you'll find a full-size Pop-A-Shot dual basketball hoop, filled with mini basketballs and is always ready for a quick game. Especially when Melvin is in the office. Across the hall, outside of Evan's office, you'll find a putting mat with putters and golf balls, available for anyone to use to help recharge before the next meeting or phone call.

Then find your way to the common area next to Tina's office. You can't miss it because it is in the middle of all the great people and it smells delicious because of all the homemade goodies that Angela, Christina, Roxann, Aisha, Veronica, and others brought in for the team to enjoy.

When you see all of this pomp and circumstance for the first time, you wonder if this is a regular type of thing. Then you get the privilege of being part of the family and you get to come back for several years, and you realize this is not only a regular thing, this is an everyday type of thing.

At that moment, you'll start to realize that their insane success with employee engagement scores and call-center retention isn't really an accident. In fact, one of their sites has an attrition rate of less than four percent. In a world where forty percent is closer to the norm...

Four percent?

More Proof

What do you do when you see outliers like this? Your curiosity forces you to ask this question... What do you all like so much about this culture?

Rob: Chris is my guy, he always puts people first.

Tina: Well, after 13 years it is family first around here. Chris has my back and treats me like I matter. Also, it is important to Chris that all of us are having fun. He really wants to help people enjoy their work and make their lives better. He's done that for me.

Jason: It's all about taking care of one another, we treat each like family. We have good days and we have bad days, but most importantly we take care of each other so that we can take care of our customers. This sounds cliché and people often forget leadership can be very simple, it's all about how you treat people.

Chris (in his own words): Two words, Family & Care. We find the right people, and do the right thing at the right time. Always focus on the person and what they need. We use this approach to help our people both internally, and externally.

Family & Work?

After the craziness of COVID settled down, I invested time to reflect on all the people that helped our little company beat the challenges of 2020. I sent Chris a note, saying thank you. Here's another direct quote from Chris: "I appreciate the note. It was nice to hear that I helped when you needed it. That's what family is about."

Chris and I are not really family. We don't share the same bloodline, or siblings, or relatives, or parents. We live almost 2,000 miles apart. But he includes me and about 1,000 other people in the family. Do you have anyone in your life like that? I hope you do. It is empowering to be a part of something bigger than yourself. My experience with Chris and his team led me to believe there is some truth to Simon Sinek's quote:

"When we feel sure they will keep us safe, we will march behind them and work tirelessly to see their visions come to life and proudly call ourselves their followers."

In the end, what can we learn from Chris and the culture he and his leaders have built? A lot.

But perhaps the thing that seems most obviously different to me, especially when I first experienced Chris's culture, is how they have intentionally designed the optimal environment...

UNLEARN CONVENIENCE

Today more than ever before, we make choices based on where things are, not because of what they are and the value they bring to us. We consistently choose the convenient options. If you don't believe me, walk around a grocery store with a three year-old... Take them down the cereal aisle, the candy aisle, the juice aisle, and the checkout lane. Did you make it out of the store alive? Of course not. It's impossible.

That experience will provide some important context for this formula: (Psychologist Kurt Lewin's Formula): $B = f(P,E)$. Behavior is a function of the Person in their Environment.[1]

This formula gives language to the idea that every choice we make is environment-dependent. For example, we know that products at eye-level tend to be purchased more than those up at the top of the shelf or down near the floor. The more obviously available a product or service is, the more likely you are to buy it (for more context on the value of visual cues and environment design, please read *Atomic Habits*).

We all know this by now. We know that we should never go into the grocery store while we are hungry. We know that we shouldn't fill our pantry with cookies if we are on a diet. We know that we shouldn't go shopping for shoes if we don't have any money to spend. We know, we know, we know.

Digital Environment Design

Today's world though, is more digital than ever. So, for Kurt Lewin's environment design formula to truly help us in the modern day, it must extend to our online focus habits.

To give us a better understanding of this, think about why almost every company will give you some sort of discount to receive your email address… They know having access to your email will yield a higher rate of future purchases. Sacrifice 10% today and have the opportunity to distract you with their products later. Simple.

Here are a few digital environment design suggestions:

- Get rid of social media.
- If you can't, limit and cautiously select what you follow.
- Block certain websites from your browser.
- Carefully select the emails you allow into your inbox.
- Cancel media subscriptions that aren't adding value.
- Delete all apps from your phone that are a distraction.
- Turn off most or all phone notifications.
- Measure your daily screen time (what gets measured usually gets managed).

In today's world, becoming a digital minimalist is one of the best ways to get ahead, but it won't take you very far if you don't design your physical environment with the right people...

UNLEARN BUSY-NESS

Remember what Chris Reese said earlier in the chapter about finding the right people? How do we do that?

Have you ever heard of the famous study in 2007 by the staff at the Washington Post? Here's what they did. They put Grammy winning violinist Joshua Bell in a Washington D.C. Metro Train Station and had him play a violin for 45 minutes. In the research, they studied pedestrians as they were rushing by without realizing that the musician playing at the entrance to the metro stop was a world-famous talent.[2]

Two days before playing in the subway, his concert sold out at a theater in Boston where the price for a seat averaged $100. He played one of the most intricate pieces ever written, all with a violin worth 3.5 million dollars. In the 45 minutes Joshua Bell played his violin outside, only six people stopped and stayed for a while. Around twenty people gave him money, but continued to walk at their normal pace. He collected a grand total of $32.

This behavioral psychology research helps us ask several important questions that correlate to life and influence. Here are two of them:

1. Do we recognize the greatness right in front of us?
2. If so, do we stop to appreciate it?

As it turns out, most of us are not nearly as perceptive to our environment as we might think we are. Think about how many people walked by Joshua Bell on that day, and only six really stopped. Heck, he was playing with a 3.5 million-dollar violin.

Great story. Why are you telling me this? What does this have to do with influence? Just stop to think about it honestly for a second. Could that have been you walking past Joshua Bell? Or even better, do you intentionally stop to appreciate the talent that is right in front of you? Has there ever been a time where you didn't even recognize the greatness of one of your family-members or one of your team-members?

In our Maximize Value Engagement research, we found that the number one reason people want to leave and find a new job... Lack of recognition and appreciation from their immediate manager.

And why are we in a hurry all the time? Where would we all be going that we couldn't stop to make time and appreciate the genius that is right in front of us? In chapter two, we talked about saving time on our calendars for firefighting. As a friendly reminder, recognizing the greatness of the people around us is exactly the type of "fire" that we should be finding time to fight.

I'm reminded of the brilliant philosopher and master strategist, Ferris Bueller and his famous quote: "Life moves pretty fast. If you don't stop and look around once in a while, you could miss it."

Which ultimately brings me to the point of this timely message... Perhaps. Just maybe. I wonder if it is possible that the best thing that we've learned from the global pandemic is if you don't take time to appreciate the great people that are already around you, you might not have the chance to do it later.

Don't let their obituary be the thing that forces you to acknowledge and talk about the greatness of the people around you...

LEARN VALUES

Speaking of obituaries, have you ever read through an obituary of someone you knew and they were saying all kinds of nice things about how involved, caring, generous, sweet, and kind they were? Then, you were forced to scroll back up to the top of the article to confirm whether or not you are still reading about the right person? Turns out you were still reading about the correct person, but the person being described was not being accurately portrayed.

Without naming names, I've done that before. And that was the moment I realized that I better live in such a way that they don't have to lie at my funeral or fabricate my obituary. And I am convinced that the only way to make that happen is to live intentionally. The only way to live an intentional life is to realize what you value most. Why? Values drive behavior. Values catalyze action. Show me your calendar and your bank account and I'll show you what you value. Where you invest (or waste) your energy, time, and money are the best indicators of what matters most to you.

To me, it seems quite remarkable when I think about how many people have never made time to pause and consider what they value. Seriously, after serving thousands of people, why do so many seem confused about what they value most? I can say that assertively because one of the most commonly requested topics we deliver for our clients is a module we call Branding. In the module, we walk through a four-step process on how to build your personal and professional brand. Here are the first three steps laid out in detail:

Step 1: Reverse Values

We start by identifying what you hate the most when you see it in yourself or in others. To uncover this, we put together a list of about fifty words that are off-putting to most people. For example, you'll find greed, laziness, arrogance, and dishonesty on the list. What can't you stand?

Which words do you hope are never said about you? Pick your top three from the list and explain why you dislike them so much.

The reason we start with what you can't stand is because usually the opposite is what you stand for. If greed is something you hate, then generosity is probably a high value for you. If arrogance is off-putting to you, then humility might be important to you. This line of thinking also helps us heighten our self-awareness so we can identify how we may come across with those in our personal and professional atmospheres.

Step 2: What Do You Want To Be Known For?

Next, we ask you to identify what you want to be known for. In this phase, we give you about one-hundred words from which you can choose. This forces you to think ahead to your funeral, or think about the words imprinted on your tombstone, or inked within your obituary.

If the speaker delivering your life-celebration message was only able to say three things about you, what would you want them to say? Why? If there were only three words on your tombstone, what would you want them to be? Why? In other words, we want you to think about what you represent. We know these are deep questions, but it is imperative that we unpack the answers so we can make sure to lead a life worthy of living. If we don't make time to identify what we want to be known for, surely we'll end up somewhere else.

Now, once you've identified your top three values, explain why you chose those three as being most important to you.

Step 3: What Are You Known For Now?

The next obvious question is... What are you known for now?

This is the step that requires the most courage. It also requires some social intelligence and emotional intelligence to fully understand how we come across today. In order to uncover the truth behind that, we go through one of our EQ growth techniques called the "How Do Others Experience Me Experiment" which includes three significant questions you will ask to someone you trust.

Here are the questions:

1. Generally, how am I perceived?
2. How would you describe your individual experience with me?
3. What is one thing I should change to enhance how I am perceived?

When they are answering this last question, make sure they tell you what you need to hear rather than what they think you want to hear. We all have blind spots and...

WHAT WE DON'T KNOW OFTEN KEEPS US FROM KNOWING WHAT WE NEED TO KNOW

After you receive some good answers from those questions, you'll be able to launch into step four which is all about building a unique plan to purposefully improve your reputation.

LEARN UNIQUENESS

What's wrong with you?

That's the question we are hoping they ask when we are done with this step of our branding plan.

What do you think they mean when they ask... What's wrong with you? They mean what's right with you. Why are you an outlier? Why are you different? Why is your uniqueness so evident?

When we think about the uniqueness within our branding plans, we need to think about the slight edge approach... Do the little things consistently and with excellence over time, and over time, it will add up to big results.[3]

A great example of this is Chick-Fil-A. They aren't flashy, they don't do anything dramatically memorable or outstanding. They just do the little things really well.

For example, they hire people who shower regularly. What else do they do? Their restaurants are clean. Their food quality is consistent and they say my pleasure. But, perhaps the most important thing they do is they live according to their values. If you listen to the music they play in their restaurants and consider the fact that they are closed on Sundays, you can easily see that they aren't hypocrites.

In 2018, Chick-Fil-A had an average of $4.7 million in sales per store, well above the $2.8 million for the golden M, and way more than most other peers. Did I mention that they are closed on Sundays? Of course, you already knew that. So yes, imitating Chick-Fil-A is a good start, but the next level requires a little more intentionality. [4]

As we continue to think about building our brand and identifying our values, our next step is to create a plan for closing the gap between what you want to be known for and what you are known for now. To do this, remember that:

UNIQUENESS IS THE HINGE ON WHICH THE DOOR TO MEMORABILITY SWINGS.

Definition of unique: being the only one of its kind; unlike anything else.

So, why demonstrate uniqueness? It is highly unlikely that we will ever have the most money or the most friends or the most resources. So how do we identify a competitive advantage that can compete with those who do?

The answer to that question is exactly why we need to unpack the memorable dining experience of Lambert's Café, which is my favorite slight edge experience.

I first heard about Lambert's when Suzanne and I were dating. We were in that discovery phase where you ask each other a million questions.

Chase: "What's your favorite restaurant?"

Suzanne: "I'm not sure what it's called but it's the one on the way to Orange Beach where they throw all the rolls to you."

Chase: "What?"

Suzanne: "You've never been there? Ya, they throw rolls at you from across the dining room. If you drop them, everyone sighs. If you catch a long one everyone gives you a thumbs up."

Fast forward about five years... We were on our way down to Orange Beach and I got the chance to stop at Lambert's for the first time.

As you make your way to your seat, you will notice a few interesting things. The first thing you'll see is a huge tub of apple butter at your table, which is a great start. Within minutes, the roll-guy will come around pushing a cart of hot out of the oven rolls, which are delicious by the way. The roll-guy isn't a waiter, just the all-time quarterback. I like to pretend that Lambert's goes to the NFL & MLB drafts and comes home with signed contracts from the quarterbacks and pitchers that didn't get selected by a pro team. I digress.

If you are within twenty yards of the roll-guy and you make eye contact, you are fair game for a touchdown pass. Soon after you catch as many rolls as you'd like, another server will come around and place piles of fried okra on your paper towel. Drinks are delivered in 44-ounce mugs and most entrees will be served on enormous 18-inch skillets.[5]

They have stores with branded merchandise everywhere and they've made a fortune by creating a unique experience for their market. They've become famous simply by doing a few unique things to provide a memorable experience for their audience. This should be a reminder to all of us that:

TO BE REMEMBERED
BE UNIQUE

Build your legacy roadmap around the uniqueness you bring to the world. Then go deliver your uniqueness in the service of others...

Look at that, a memorable brand has emerged!

LEARN ACCOUNTABILITY

After we've recognized our brand's identity, we need to embed ourselves into a culture of accountability. This will help us live according to our values and stay focused on what matters most.

accountability: an obligation or willingness to accept responsibility for one's actions.

Unfortunately, accountability is widely misconstrued in our world today. Even though most people don't fully understand accountability, it is a shockingly brilliant thing when we witness a system comprised of people with a willingness to accept responsibility for their actions and outcomes. This type of system is something we rarely see, but we all want to be a part of.

This may sound counter-intuitive to many, but we should set-up cultures of accountability for:

- Ourselves
- Our families
- Our industries
- Our communities
- Our organizations

The reason many people seem resistant to the establishment of a culture of accountability is because they have never seen it done well. Here are the four most important misconceptions that come with accountability:

1. Accountability is only for performance expectations, not behavioral expectations.
2. Accountability is only needed to address other people, not to address ourselves.
3. Accountability should only be used to address consequences.
4. Accountability should only be used to address our direct-reports.

Accountability is a gift and true demonstration of respect for the people around you, when done properly. Let's address these four misconceptions that come with accountability so we can start to view it the proper way. Here are the four steps to helping us change the accountability narrative:

Step 1: Clear Expectations

This step shouldn't have to be said:

BEFORE WE EVER HOLD ANYONE ACCOUNTABLE, WE NEED TO SET CLEAR EXPECTATIONS.

After traveling the world and working with all different types of organizations, we've found that most people are clear on their own performance expectations, but they have no clue about the behavioral expectations or the deliverables and focus areas of others (outside of their direct reports). This is madness.

In order to effectively hold anyone else accountable, you must have clarity around the expectations that exist for your team to be successful. This means every single player on the team needs to know and understand the key deliverables that each person is responsible for day-to-day, week-to-week, and month-to-month.

Let's change the story on this and start by working with all of your team-members to answer these three questions:

- What should team-members expect of me (the leader) both from a performance standpoint and from a behavioral standpoint?
- What should I expect from you (both performance and behavioral)?
- What should we expect from each other (peer-to-peer, up-and-down)?

This may seem like common sense to you, but in reality, common sense is not all that common anymore.

If we did step one correctly, we are ready to jump into step two…

Step 2: Self-Accountability

The second accountability paradigm that we must address is in relation to self-accountability. Candidly stated:

IF WE DON'T HOLD OURSELVES ACCOUNTABLE, WE WON'T BE ABLE TO EFFECTIVELY HOLD OTHERS ACCOUNTABLE.

For growth to happen, inventory-taking is an extremely powerful tool to apply consistently within your organization. This inventory taking needs to start with you taking a deep look into the mirror and evaluating your own outcomes. Remember, we tend to judge ourselves by our intentions and we tend to judge others by their actions. Make sure you are not only looking at your intentions, but your behaviors when assessing your current reality.

Step 3: Positive Accountability

In order to build a culture of accountability, we have to understand the fundamentals of why accountability exists within the organizational structure. Let's start by coming into agreement that most of the accountability that is done by leaders is done through a negative lens. In other words, the accountability only happens when people miss the mark on performance metrics or behavioral expectations.

Today, accountability has become more of a leadership checklist type of response, rather than acting from a place of care for your people. Let's get this straight, when we hold others accountable we are saying: I see you and I am paying attention to you. Your work matters. I value you and see great potential in you. I care too much about you to not honor your output (good or bad).

To deconstruct the misconceptions that come with accountability, we need to approach it from the proper heart posture. This will help us increase our chances of being received with optimism and gratitude instead of compliance and animosity. The main thing to change within our leadership approach is to hold people accountable when they exceed expectations. Honor them and recognize them instead of just having this conversation when they miss the mark (this also applies to parenting).

Nowhere in the definition of accountability does it say that you have an obligation to accept responsibility for your actions only when things go poorly. You can accept responsibility for your actions when amazing things happen and you exceed expectations, too. There are two sides to the coin when it comes to accountability, and a true influencer will prioritize both sides of the coin within their sphere of influence:

> **Side 1:** We will praise you, recognize you, reward you, and make you take responsibility for your actions when great things happen.

> **Side 2:** We will kindly, tactfully, and caringly hold our team-members accountable when we miss the mark.

Step 4: Peer to Peer Accountability

The last item of competence is in regards to the idea that we should only hold our direct reports accountable. This couldn't be less effective. We are a team, and we exist to win together. That's why we need to hold our peers and our managers accountable, in addition to our direct reports.

Why do we only hold our direct reports accountable? Because that's what we were taught to do and we can check that off of our leadership checklist if we do it consistently. But what about the rest of our team-members, including our managers and peers? Should we hold them accountable too? The answer is an affirmative yes.

Why would we do that? Why would we go out of our way to do something that isn't directly connected to our paycheck?

Because if we really care about our work and our team-members, then we should be honoring and recognizing each other when we go above and beyond. We should also be asking questions when we fall short of the desired outcomes. Again, why would we do this? It really comes down to a mindset of believing in the potential of our team and the members that are involved in the work we do.

Three Questions:

1. Do we believe in delivering a high-quality product to our stakeholders?
2. Do we believe in the product or service we are delivering?
3. Do we believe in the people on our team?

If we can't answer those questions with an assertive YES, it might be time to look for a new opportunity. If we do believe in those three things, then this peer-to-peer accountability thought-pattern can be a powerful tool to help us build better cultures.

CHAPTER SUMMARY: CULTURE

The word "culture" was derived from the Latin word cultus, which means to care, or to cultivate.

Care: look after, provide for the needs of. Cultivate: foster the growth of.

Use these six techniques to look after, provide for, and foster the growth of the people in your sphere of influence:

1. **Unlearn Metrics:** Put people first and help your people enjoy their work. When you do, the numbers seem to fall into place.

2. **Unlearn Convenience:** We must design our ecosystems in a way that helps us make the best decision, not the easiest decision.

3. **Unlearn Busy-ness:** Are we too busy to stop and recognize the greatness of the people who are right in front of us?

4. **Learn Values:** Let's intentionally identify our values and live according to them so they don't have to fabricate our obituaries.

5. **Learn Uniqueness:** To be remembered, be unique. Let's build our legacy-roadmap around the uniqueness we bring to the world.

6. **Learn Accountability:**
   - First: we need to set clear expectations.
   - Second: we need to hold ourselves accountable.
   - Third: we need to hold our team-members accountable when we miss the mark and when things go well.
   - And finally, put a framework in place so that all team-members can hold each-other accountable.

CHAPTER 6

LEARNING

"The quality of your mind is the quality of your life."

— Naval Ravikant

UNLEARN PROCUREMENT

Who you learn from is more important than what they teach you...

Please don't get me wrong on this, what they teach you is extremely important, too. It's just that their experiential knowledge weighs far more than the lessons they share. With that in mind, I am shocked at how many travel agents there are in this world.

Just stop for a second and think about what travel agents get paid to do... They get paid to send you to places they probably have never been.[1]

When Andrew, Sarah, and I were planning our trip to Africa, we used a travel agent, but at that time in my life I wasn't smart enough to ask the only necessary question to the lady helping us. To me, the door of success in travel-agent-land hinges upon one simple question: Have you been there before? If the answer is no, move on. If the answer is yes, feel free to follow-up with: How recently?

With the advent of the internet, these travel agents are able to disguise themselves with a little credibility. In leadership, we see this level of hypocrisy all over the place. Leaders telling their people to fix the widget, but they have no idea how to fix it themselves.

Entrepreneurial Travel Agents

One of the most defining "moments" of my life was centered around the months leading up to launching Maximize Value. About six months prior to going all-in on this dream, I asked my friends for their advice. After a few dozen conversations, I found that there were four different types of people in my little world:

1. Doubters: The people that didn't believe in me. I was smart enough to have never asked them a single question about their opinion.
2. Wimps: The people that did believe in me, but they were scared by the thought of signing the front of a paycheck instead of the back.
3. Champions: The people that did believe in me, and it didn't matter what I was doing, they were going to be champions for the cause. Suzanne, My Mom, and My Sister were a few that fell into this category.
4. Mentors: The people that did believe in me and they actually had the experience to provide relevant advice.

Personally, I found that many people fell into the second category. Quite a few people who are terrified of leaving their comfort zone of a paycheck that they try to scare you into believing that the security of working for someone else is better than the risk of being an entrepreneur. I was shocked at how many people knew and recited the statistic that most businesses fail within the first five years. If I had a dollar for every time I heard: You know Chase, it takes two to three years for a business to be profitable... I probably would have been profitable before launching the company.

After talking to all these travel agents in my life, the fear of others was starting to spill over into my brain. Instead of being scared and letting my anxiety control me, I sat down with seven of my friends who were successful entrepreneurs. Some of them played in the nine-figure ballpark. Chip, Chris, Greg, JC, Jeff, Leo, & Mike. I asked them all one question: What is your advice for me?

Do you know how many of them told me not to do it? None of them. Do you know how many recited the statistics about how hard it is to be an entrepreneur? None of them. Every single one of them encouraged me to do it and they all said it would be one of the best decisions that I would ever make. And, they were right. But even beyond their insight and encouragement, they all offered their free help with some form of this language... Keep me posted and let me know how I can help you get started.

All of these people I talked to were my friends. They have good hearts, some of them just didn't have any credibility to speak on this subject. They should have said "I don't know, I've never done it before." This world would be a much better place if we could all learn to say I don't know.

But it is not their fault. It is 100% my fault. Why? Because I asked for their opinions...

I SHOULD HAVE NEVER ASKED MY TRAVEL AGENT FRIENDS ABOUT PLANNING A TRIP TO A PLACE THEY'VE NEVER BEEN

Along those lines, it is remarkable to me how many people in this world are so scared of something that they desire other people to be scared of the same thing. This makes them feel way better about their unnecessary insecurity. Much of the world works like this, by the way. Some of the stuff we are going through in our world right now is the perfect example of how we can easily scare the world into being scared with us. Fear is a tremendous motivator, which we will talk more about later in this chapter.

At Maximize Value, we pride ourselves on the fact that no one is allowed to deliver training on a particular module if they don't have experiential proficiency with the content. The world would be a better place if they took a page out of our playbook, but it is only getting worse with social media. In the end, this is a friendly reminder for all of us to not be travel agents and to not take advice from travel agents. And let me say it just one more time...

WHO YOU LEARN FROM IS MORE IMPORTANT THAN WHAT THEY TEACH YOU.

UNLEARN NONSENSE

I'm not sure if the quality of your mind is the quality of your life, but I do know that the quality of your mind dictates the quality of your life. As we consider the value of that truth, it might be beneficial for us to understand how the mind actually works.

To help us get started, there is a CIA interrogation tool called the Alice in Wonderland technique. This approach can help explain the importance of how we should demonstrate influence inside of our organizations, and out. In essence, here's how it works: Two or three interrogators are working together. When the subject enters the room, the first interrogator asks a totally nonsensical question, one which seems straightforward, and possibly meaningful, but is essentially nonsensical. If the interrogatee tries to answer or not, it doesn't matter.[2]

Then the second interrogator follows up with another question, and may even interrupt the interrogatee's answer with a totally unrelated and equally nonsensical question. At times, there will be two or more questions asked simultaneously.

The cadence, pitch, tonality, and volume of the interrogators' voices will have no pattern or congruence. There will be no correlation in the type of questions, nor do the questions themselves relate logically to each other. Then, they repeat this approach for several weeks or even months.[3]

Why would this be an effective way to uncover sensitive criminal information?

I promise, I'll explain it, just let me provide some neuroscience context first.

An Introduction to Neuroscience

You don't have to study Maslow to understand that survival is the primary desire of the human brain. If that doesn't make sense, then drop this book and go lock yourself in a room with a hungry lion. If anything is militating against this primal desire to survive today, then we won't be able to focus on anything else.[4]

The second desire of the human brain is a little more complex, but even more important to understand in the context of influencing others. What does this say:

I lvoe tihs praagarhp wthi pylochsgyoy ctonnet

Isn't that interesting? How are we able to decipher that jumbled mess?

We can unscramble those letters because our brains are these remarkable, built-in prediction, algorithmic machines that reside under our skulls.[5] They are constantly and subconsciously trying to anticipate what is going to happen next. This subconscious forecasting helps us understand that:

THE SECOND DESIRE OF THE HUMAN BRAIN IS TO BE ABLE TO PREDICT.

So why do we respond the way we do in certain situations? Well, our brains and therefore our behaviors are driven primarily by two main impact systems. The reward system and the threat system. Our brains know that the first priority is to survive, thus we almost automatically seek to avoid threats, and find rewards. But of the two responses, the minimize threats (or dangers) response is much more important to us.

Just think back to the last time you got an email at work criticizing one of your projects or deliverables. Now think back to the time you got an email publicly praising you for your production or success. Which one had more of a long-term impact on you? Why do you think that is?

The negative email was probably more impactful because our brains are simply trying to predict what will happen next so they can keep us out of harm's way. If we get to experience pleasure (dopamine) in the process, that's great – but survival is what our brains are primarily seeking. With that negative email in mind, we know that anything causing us to change can be challenging for us.

Can we all just say it together… People hate change… Change is hard.

You've heard both of those sayings a bunch, but are they true? I personally believe that:

PEOPLE DON'T HATE CHANGE. THEY JUST HATE BEING CHANGED… THERE IS A DIFFERENCE.

As influencers, when we introduce change, this activates the threat system in the brain. This negative response simply means that blood flows away from our prefrontal cortex, which is very important for thinking and making logical decisions, and goes to the part of the brain that gets us ready for fight or flight.[6]

Ultimately, this means that our thinking is impaired, and we have less control over our emotions. In the end, we see our world as dangerous, and our performance drops off because we are stressed and we can't focus on production.

To phrase it with more simplicity:

UNCERTAINTY IS THE DRIVER OF MOST STRESS

Now that we understand the brain a little bit, let's bring it all the way back to the Alice in Wonderland CIA technique. Why does it work? Because people would rather divulge sensitive information than live in a world that doesn't make any sense.

So, make your model predictable. If you don't make it predictable, you are unintentionally making it stressful. Make it make sense. Both for yourself, and for others.

One of the best ways to help make it make sense is to learn how to apply a useful mental model...

UNLEARN ACCEPTANCE

If you don't love your life, it is probably because someone else influenced your life more than you did. Let me explain...

Most influencers will lead you astray from time to time. Not intentionally, but it will happen. Almost every single one of my favorite thought leaders has done or said something publicly that I fundamentally disagree with. That doesn't mean that they aren't brilliant thinkers, it just means that we disagree on at least one thing. If we are honest though, we all do and say things that we disagree with from time-to-time. I don't want you to take anything I say in this book as absolute truth. Instead, you should evaluate the validity of what I am delivering to you and be able to quantify if there is any value in my words. If so, take it and seek to apply it in your own life. If not, please drop it to the ground and let it burn. We should never just believe something or value something just because one of our favorite thought leaders recommended it to us. And that's exactly why:

EVEN AFTER WE CAREFULLY SELECT WHO WE LEARN FROM, WE NEED TO LEARN HOW TO SYNTHESIZE AND DISCERN.

synthesize*:* combine (a number of things) into a coherent whole.

discernment: the ability to judge well.

Synthesis and discernment are so important because of all the noise that exists in our world today… And the unfortunate reality is that the most degenerate in our society tend to shout with the loudest voices. But who cares about their degeneracy? To each his own… Right?

Wrong! That's the idiom many people use to justify their ignorance of these egregious situations… How do you think that's going for us? The "to each his own" phraseology is fine if you don't want to be an influencer, but this is a book about influence, and real influencers care about these situations because we ultimately value the wellbeing of those in our spheres.

Some might say that they don't care about the degeneracy that someone else engages in, as long as it doesn't affect them. The problem, though, is that we live in communities where we are all connected to each other in some sense of the word. For example (on a larger scale), if someone in our community becomes a murderer, it impacts the entire community. If someone in our community becomes a drug-dealer, it impacts the rest of us. If someone in our community becomes a hoarder and allows their property to become run-down, it impacts the property value of the entire neighborhood (on a much smaller scale). All three of these situations make the environment more menacing for the rest of the community.

This is a significant problem because today we are seeing those without a moral compass yelling as if they deserve to be accepted into and worshiped within our societies, neighborhoods, and organizations. In other words, the murderers, the drug-dealers, and the hoarders want us to welcome them in so they can destroy our communities. They come in, do a little demolition, then go make friends with others and start propagating the message that it is acceptable to be like them. This cycle keeps repeating itself over and over again... Until true influencers stand against this lunacy and stand up for what is right.

So, how do we that? How do we consistently stand for what is right? Can we simply give advice on how to behave and how to live? No...

PEOPLE GENERALLY DON'T FOLLOW OUR ADVICE, THEY FOLLOW OUR EXAMPLE.

Therefore, when you demonstrate strength and boldness, it seems to empower others to do the same.

With that in mind, we can:
- Choose to make decisions that are noble and virtuous.
- Choose to build the fortitude necessary to stand for good.
- Choose to live in a way that is compelling and attractive.
- Choose to stand against the reprobate behavior that annihilates our communities.

Let me be clear: true influencers exist to help those in need and be a source of light wherever they are. But there is a big difference between you influencing these people and letting them influence you. Thus, we need to make sure we are the ones doing the influencing, not the other way around.

Whether we like it or not, even Jesus of Nazareth confronted the foolishness in the local community. How is it possible that Jesus is often referred to as the epitome of love and is simultaneously talked about as the most influential person to ever walk on the planet, yet called people fools and overturned tables in the temple?

Some people choose to ignore that part of the text because they have a hard time understanding how this type of interaction could be loving or even influential in a positive way, so let me explain... His demonstration of love came in the form of confronting people who were trying to enslave others with their deceitfulness. One example of this is in the book of Matthew in the New Testament:

> *Woe to you, scribes and Pharisees, hypocrites,*
> *because you travel around on sea and land to make one*
> *proselyte; and when he becomes one, you make him*
> *twice as much a son of hell as yourselves.* [7]

That situation from two-thousand years ago is very similar to what we see in our organizations or even in our communities today. This type of interaction is the perfect example of where a good mental model would be able to help us. Instead of just accepting this behavior and allowing it to exist around us, we can help ourselves and others pursue a path to a more sensible approach.

What is a mental model? In essence, a mental model helps you understand how things work and they ultimately help you make better decisions.[8] There are hundreds of good mental models out there, you just need to find which one helps you increase your winning percentage the most. Here's one of my favorites...

The Regret Minimization Mental Model

The regret minimization mental model is just a spin on applying the law of opportunity cost to how we make decisions. So, what is the law of opportunity cost?

Definition from my Managerial Economics Textbook: The loss of potential gain from other alternatives when one alternative is chosen.

Definition from Me: The short-term loss you intentionally take to win in the long-run (or vice versa).

Examples of Daily Opportunity Cost Decisions We Make:

- Do I choose the pain of potentially upsetting the person I need to coach, or do I choose the pain of letting this go and letting their bad attitude become a major source of toxicity for our organization (similar to the example of neighborhood drug-dealers or hoarders, but within an organizational setting).

- Do I choose the pain of potentially being criticized because I shared my idea, or do I choose the pain of feeling like I have lived an insignificant life because I kept all my ideas to myself?

- Do I choose the pain of going into debt because I bought a car I couldn't really afford or do I choose the pain of saving cash and buying a car without a loan?

Understanding opportunity cost is not only significant for economics, but also for how we individually invest our time and energy. One simple thing we can do to help us improve our decision-making is to look at how we design our environments with effective triggers and cues. Ideally, the triggers around us should visually act as a catalyst to help us make better choices. That's why, in our master bathroom you'll see a bottle of Calvin Klein Eternity cologne. In my SUV and in my office, you'll find pictures of my Dad located where you can't miss them. On my right wrist I always wear a wristband with an important word or phrase on it (examples: care, legacy, maximize, servant, positivity only). All of those things are visual reminders to help me make decisions that will benefit me and the people I love in the long-term.

In that same vein, we have a gym in our basement, nothing fancy. Treadmill, stair-master, bench press, squat rack, free weights, and resistance bands. In the gym you'll see two large, framed posters with some of my favorite inspirational quotes...

One of them is from Jim Rohn and it says:

"WE MUST ALL SUFFER FROM ONE OF TWO PAINS: THE PAIN OF DISCIPLINE OR THE PAIN OF REGRET."

This quote is simply a reminder to use this mental model to help drive my behavior. Am I choosing the pain of discipline or regret? Short term loss, long-term win?

Applying This Mental Model

Throughout 2017, I invested a bunch of time building training content for our company. One of the most memorable pieces of content came from when I was studying motivation and ended up reading several research articles about regrets in life and how thinking about potential regrets could be used to motivate yourself to act.

Most of the data that I found will lead you to this conclusion:

IF YOU ASK THOSE THAT ARE ON THE VERGE OF DEATH WHAT THEY REGRET OR WOULD HAVE DONE DIFFERENTLY, THEY GENERALLY SAY THAT THEY HOLD ONTO MORE REGRETS OF INACTION RATHER THAN OF ACTION. [9]

Regret Examples:

- I regret not starting my own business

- I regret not spending more time with my loved ones

- I regret not publishing my book

- I regret not coaching my daughter's soccer team

- I regret not traveling more with my wife

I quickly realized that this approach appealed to my particular motives, and I would be able to use this as a catalyst for action for the rest of my life... Here is the process for how to use this mental model:

Step 1: Define my potential future regrets. What are the worst scenarios I can imagine? List a few.

Step 2: What can I do consistently to prevent or decrease the likelihood of these things happening?

Step 3: What will I do today to help prevent the problem from happening?

Step 4: What will it cost me if I do nothing? If I avoid this action or decision and others like it, what might my life look like in three months, one year, five years (emotionally, financially, physically, etc.)?

Personal Example: Applying This Mental Model

Potential Regret: Not being able to be a Grandpa (my Dad never got to be a Grandpa).

Consistent Preventative Actions: Workout six times per week and eat heart healthy food so that my cholesterol, blood sugar, and blood pressure are under control.

Today's Preventative Actions: Take a multi-vitamin, green smoothie for breakfast, run one mile, lift weights (today is leg day), and eat heart healthy foods.

What Will It Cost Me If I Do Nothing: Possibly the opportunity to be a Grandpa. If I avoid or ignore my health, I could have a heart attack in my 40s and I won't be able to coach my kids' soccer teams or walk my daughters down the aisle.

Why does this work for me? Most people know that we make decisions emotionally and we use logic to justify them. Becoming an entrepreneur was an emotional decision that I justified with this logic. Publishing this book was an emotional decision that I justified using this logic. Giving money to charity is an emotional decision that we justify using this logic.

Suzanne: Have we ever regretted being generous? Nope...

That question makes the decision easy for us and that's exactly what a good mental model will do for you. If you don't have a mental model you use to synthesize information or to help you discern, you could one day find yourself checking out of a grocery store, looking at a magazine cover with a tagline saying: *"The Benefits of Daily Alcohol Consumption"*... And you could be deceived into thinking it has validity.

IF YOU LEARN TO SYNTHESIZE AND DISCERN, YOU WON'T JUST BLINDLY BELIEVE EVERYTHING YOU'RE TOLD WITHOUT EXAMINING IT, LIKE MANY PEOPLE DO.

LEARN TO LEARN

Everyone wants to be sharp, but only a few will invest the time to sharpen. Sharpness is vitally important in the scope of influence because of this Venn diagram:

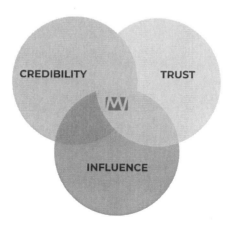

IF I DO NOT FIND YOU TO BE CREDIBLE, I WILL NOT TRUST YOU. IF I DO NOT TRUST YOU, I WILL NOT LET YOU INFLUENCE ME.

When you really break down what credibility means to people, it means intelligence. It is not necessarily what it says in the dictionary, but if you ask people about their interpretation of credibility, this is essentially what it means to them. In other words, if you are credible, they perceive you to be an intelligent expert in that particular space.

Unfortunately, very few will actually tell you that they don't find you to be credible, they just demonstrate their lack of trust in you through noncompliance. You might start to see this play out when they don't buy into your ideas or maybe you see them asking your peers for advice instead of you. In essence, they don't look to you to be their solution finder.

You can partially verify your own level of credibility by looking at the size of your paycheck (this is only one of several different indicators regarding your level of credibility). Are people willing to pay for your expertise? If so, you probably have a little credibility. If not, you can do the math. In the end, the reason that your paycheck is a pretty good indicator of credibility is because it is a byproduct of your ability to solve important problems for people.

If you are struggling to wrap your mind around this, then study why Administrative Assistants make less per hour than most Managers. Or, why does a Paralegal make less than an Attorney?

THE MORE EXPERTISE YOU DEVELOP, THE MORE YOU ARE ABLE TO SOLVE PROBLEMS FOR OTHERS. WHEN YOU SOLVE MORE PROBLEMS, YOU WIN MORE MONEY. WHEN YOU SOLVE MORE DIFFICULT PROBLEMS, YOUR TIME BECOMES MORE VALUABLE (SIMPLE SUPPLY & DEMAND).

That's why Grant Cardone's keynotes are $250,000.00 for an hour or two of insight and inspiration. [10] He is more than just a credible expert in his space, he is one of just a few people on the planet that can help people solve some very complex problems. In other words, he has earned the right to charge whatever he wants because of how much demand he has created for his time and expertise.

In the world of influence, it is true that people tend to follow the lead of credible experts... So be one. But how?

Warren Buffett answered a question similar to this when he was in a room with more than 100 students from Columbia University. One of the students raised his hand and asked Buffett for his thoughts on the best way to prepare for an investing career... After thinking for a moment, Buffett pulled out a stack of papers and trade reports he had brought with him and said, "Read 500 pages like this every day. That's how knowledge works. It builds up, like compound interest. All of you can do it, but I guarantee not many of you will do it." [11]

Warren is right, pretty much everyone in our modern world over the age of six can read, but very few will actually invest the time to read every day. Didn't the New Testament say something like this?

WIDE IS THE GATE AND BROAD IS THE ROAD THAT LEADS TO LAZINESS, AND MANY ENTER THROUGH IT. BUT SMALL IS THE GATE AND NARROW THE ROAD THAT LEADS TO BRILLIANCE, AND ONLY A FEW FIND IT. [12]

OK, maybe my context on that last part is off a little bit (wink) but I believe my intentional misquote to be pretty well-represented in our world today (if you don't agree, please thoroughly review Chapter 2).

If we just breakdown the bottom circle of the Venn diagram, it is really just a derivative of your inputs and outputs (for more context, please review the chart in chapter one). Inputs, meaning what you consume to gain credibility. Outputs, meaning how you distribute your credibility to your world. So, how do we intentionally build credibility? Let's revisit what Warren said and start by reading daily...

Why Read Books in the 21st Century?

My Senior year of High School was amazing... During our first soccer game of the year, Greg Jordan stole the ball, passed to me, and we scored eight seconds into the game. Michael Collins, one of our best friends growing up, yelled from the stands and told me I was on pace to score 13,500 goals that year. By halftime, that number faded quickly, but pretty much everything was still great in my little world... I had already committed to playing at the University of Louisville, and the future seemed bright, but there was one thing that sucked about my senior year and it made me realize why I needed to get my act together. This is the story of how I recognized my cognitive inadequacy, and the story of what happened next...

It all started with the fact that I couldn't get into Duke.

But my sister did get into Duke, and she got a full scholarship to attend. Why couldn't I get in? We lived in the same house, had the same loving parents, had many of the same friends, and enjoyed most of the same hobbies... Maybe this conversation I had with my Grandma Kreger each Thanksgiving will help provide some context:

Grandma: What books would you like for Christmas?

Chase: I don't want any, Grandma. I just want some Titleist golf balls.

Grandma: Well, what do you like to read?

Chase: I don't like to read.

Grandma: Well, if you were going to read something, what would you like to learn?

Chase: I don't know Grandma, maybe sports.

So, every year in my stocking I would find a book about sports. I completed zero of them. While I spent my life playing sports and not reading, my sister was simultaneously accumulating "Reader of the Month" awards from the library every summer. Maybe that explains the Duke admissions situation?

Maybe that scenario also explains why it is fair to say:

"THE MAN WHO DOES NOT READ HAS NO ADVANTAGE OVER THE MAN WHO CANNOT READ." – MARK TWAIN

The good news is, in 2009 I fell in love with reading and I recently crossed over my 500th book milestone. This is really not impressive because some of those books were written by Dr. Seuss. But truly, the number of books you complete is a worthless measurement – it really doesn't matter how many books you read. What matters is how you change your behavior because of what you learned. Please don't confuse reading with action. We are judged by others based on how we act, not how we think. Without changing how you act, you just think you are smart, which is even worse.

Today, we always set aside $2,000 in our annual Maximize Value budget for books. After investing about $10,000 in books over the last five years, I can say without hesitation, that some books will help you generate an insane return on your investment, but it is up to you to go and find the value within the pages.

Reading one book won't turn you into a genius, but reading daily can turn your mind into a modern-day superpower. Why?

READING ALLOWS YOU TO DOWNLOAD THE MINDSETS OF SOME OF THE MOST ADMIRABLE THINKERS WHO HAVE EVER WALKED ON THIS PLANET.

So, let's start reading and using what we learn before it is too late...

Use It or Lose It

To understand how to use it, we must go back to the fact that if we don't learn to use parts of our brains, we will lose them. Seriously...

"Neurons, neural systems, and the brain change depending on use. Just as the synaptic connections increase and strengthen through repetition, so the connections weaken and wither if we don't use them. The brain takes a use it or lose it approach: if neurons and synapses are not used, the brain prunes them away."
– Hilary Scarlett

This brain pruning technique is probably a byproduct of the fact that our brains are looking to take shortcuts to conserve energy.[13] These shortcuts can help us in a positive way, but they can also hurt us in a very negative way. This energy conservation motive also provides some explanation as to why we are vulnerable to the degenerate influences we discussed earlier in the chapter. Why are we vulnerable? Because our brains are susceptible to taking the less demanding route and we often make decisions without thinking through them more comprehensively. These choices tend to hurt us in the long-term... Why?

SHORTCUTS ARE HARDLY EVER SHORTCUTS

Is that true? Well, one example of a seemingly insignificant modern-day shortcut that we often take is to type out our thoughts on a computer. Why do we choose the typed version over the handwritten version? Because typing is "easier" and faster than handwriting with a pen and paper. From an overall retention standpoint, this too has proven to be less effective... Says who?

In 2014, Pam Mueller and Daniel Oppenheimer studied 67 students from Princeton University, each of which were assigned to watch a TED Talk. Half of them were to take notes with a laptop, and the other half were to take notes with a pen and paper. After watching the video, they were then taken to a lab to complete two different five-minute distractor tests. After about thirty minutes of elapsed time (from the time of finishing the TED Talk) they were asked to come back and answer factual-recall questions and conceptual-application questions about the video they watched. The results:

> "On factual-recall questions, the participants of both note-taking techniques performed equally well across conditions. However, on conceptual-application questions, laptop note-takers performed significantly worse than the longhand note-taking participants."[14]

In other words, the easier way has proven to be the harder way. The path of less resistance turned into the path of more resistance. Shocking.

Combine Reading & Writing

Bertrand Russell famously said:

"MOST MEN WOULD RATHER DIE THAN THINK, AND MANY DO."

Is that true? I don't know if it has always been true and I don't even know if it was true when Bertrand made the statement, but you can see clear evidence of it today when you watch how many people follow authority before they make time to think for themselves.

How is this possibly a problem that exists in our world today? We have access to more information than ever before… And maybe that's the beginning of the problem.

Our brains are similar to computers in the idea that computers have their own machine code, which tells them what to do (and computers can only do what they are told to do). Similarly, our brains can only process the information we provide for them. In that same vein, our brains are remarkable in the fact that they have the ability to process tremendous amounts of information, but they don't have the ability to discern the difference between what is important and what is trivial. We are single-handedly responsible for programming our brains in that way. Here is how computer coding and brain coding can be similar:

COMPUTER CODING:

Coding a computer is the process of using a programming language to get a computer to behave how you want it to. Being a good programmer is primarily about knowing how to tell a computer to act.

BRAIN CODING:

Coding a human brain is the process of using your intentional consumption to get your mind to behave how you want it to. Being a good influencer is primarily about knowing how to tell your brain to act.

Perhaps the best evidence of our ineffectiveness with coding our own brains is obvious when we look at our shortening attention spans and our diminishing comprehension ability… How do we change this?

Steve Graham and Michael Hebert wondered the same thing, so they conducted some important research in their work, *Writing to Read.* In their study, they conducted several experiments which ultimately found evidence for how writing after reading can improve reading retention and comprehension. In review, they say the data shows that extended writing has a strong and consistently positive impact on reading comprehension. The positive outcome they found can be outlined in this summary:

"Extended writing produced greater comprehension gains than simply reading the text, reading and rereading it, reading and studying it, reading and discussing it, and receiving reading instruction." [15]

In summary, the ultimate trifecta when it comes to learning is:

1. Read first, and read daily. This habit helps you on the path to earning with your mind instead of your time. It might even help you get into Duke (make sure to avoid reading anything from a travel agent).

2. Write second, and write after you read. Writing is formalized thinking and it helps you clarify your thoughts. If you read and don't write, your comprehension and retention will suffer.

3. Teach (or speak) third. Teaching others what you've learned is the definitive measurement of your comprehension, and that's where we are going next...

LEARN TO TEACH (& TEACH TO LEARN)

Over the last decade, I've been training people on the idea that the shortest path to trust-building is a deep understanding of what the stakeholder needs. Thus, when we learn to ask thought-provoking and open-ended questions, we will discover how to best serve our audience. This is usually valuable insight.

But what if they don't know what they need or even what they want?

In that scenario (which is unfortunately prevalent), the better approach might be to teach them what they need, or what they want. When we recognize that most people don't know what they need or want, we realize that our success in influence is not about understanding their world as well as they understand it themselves. Instead, we start to comprehend that we can influence our sphere at a much higher level by actually knowing their world better than they know it themselves. Then, we can use this insight to teach them what they don't know, but should know.

You've heard before that the pastor learns more than the congregation. The author learns more than the reader. The speaker learns more than the audience. The teacher learns more than the student. We know this to be true, don't we?

I knew all that in my brain, but I still never had ambitions to be a teacher. Then came June of 2012 when I heard these words: "Chase, we need to talk. We need our money back. Under no circumstance will we continue on with the program."

The company we were in partnership with was a well-known company and the lady in charge of overseeing our partnership was sharp, kind, and unfortunately – she was right.

My paycheck at the time was made up of a small base salary with quarterly commission checks. The commission checks made up the majority of my income and the commission structure was calculated based on my quarterly collections. So, I sold this big deal, collected the money, and then of course calculated the amount that I was going to receive on my next commission check, and I was excited... Until I wasn't.

That was the moment in time I made the decision that if I was ever going to lose diaper money because of something going wrong, it was going to be because of the guy in the mirror. While playing soccer in college, I learned that I would rather be on the field when we lose than on the bench. It is fine if you blame me for the loss, but I want to be on the field.

So, I had to learn to be a teacher. I didn't grow up wanting to be a teacher, quite the opposite. Like most people, I was scared of public speaking and I never felt like I was the smartest person in the room. I didn't feel like I had the credibility to teach anyone anything, except for maybe how to play soccer.

This obsession for learning to teach was birthed out of necessity. Which is a fantastic platform from which we should all launch. When you truly need something, the intensity and velocity with which you travel increases. And that's exactly what happened. The next month, I signed up to go back to graduate school and get my MBA. Then I enrolled in all kinds of certification programs to learn how to teach and I immediately started delivering free workshops to anyone and any organization that would have me (one highlight memory was teaching at Golden Corral).

And, yes, I wasn't an outlier to Emerson's quote when he said: "All great speakers were bad speakers first." I was terrible, but I kept putting one foot in front of the next. And, it didn't feel like it was too much of a sacrifice at the time because Suzanne was committed to going back to school too, so we just decided to do the whole graduate school thing together. No kids at the time, so we knew it would be a few years of short-term investing for a long-term gain. And we were right.

The moral of the story is that much of my progress in the business realm was truly birthed out of a place of recognizing my need for learning, and more specifically, learning to teach. We all have the same need, whether we recognize it or not. And most don't.

So how can we make this more of a priority? Both on a personal level, but also for the people we serve?

A Learning Framework

Every good company out there has a Position Description for every role in the organization. Within those outlines, we have frameworks for deliverables, quotas, production, profitability, quality, and other minutiae. What you won't find on most of those detailed documents is a Positional Area of Focus around Learning and Professional Development.

When it comes to learning, the first step to take is to recognize your need for it. Once you recognize that mandate, then we can move to step two which is managing it. We know what gets measured usually gets managed, so we have to measure it. How do we do that?

Here are a few helpful Quarterly Review Questions:

1. What books have you completed over the last three months? Please explain the most important lessons you learned from your reading.
2. What professional development initiatives have you completed in the past quarter (seminars, workshops, classes, on-site training, peer training, management coaching, or mentoring). Please explain how these have benefited you.
3. In relation to your position with serving our company, what major things have you learned that will help you take your results to the next level? How did you learn these new things? What advice would you give to others on our team so they can also learn these things and apply them to help us grow our business?

After we successfully create a structure for measuring and managing our learning, we can move into our next phase of learning which is to do it with velocity...

LEARN WITH VELOCITY

We've all heard before that the road to hell is paved with good intentions. It has always been true, but never more evident than it is today. After watching the world evolve before our eyes in less than a year, we've all witnessed good intentions kill a lot of jobs, businesses, families, and even people.

Which brings us to the truth that understanding a concept intellectually matters zero if we don't put the learning into action. Why? We aren't evaluated based on our knowledge or intentions, we are evaluated by our behavior.

James speaks to the depth of a similar idea when talking about the connection between faith and action. I've made a slight adjustment to the verses in the New Testament and this is what it would sound like if we replaced the word faith with knowledge:

> *What good is it if someone claims to have knowledge but has no action? Can such knowledge save them? Knowledge by itself, if it is not accompanied by action is dead. Show me your knowledge without actions and I will show you my knowledge by my actions.*[16]

Today, the challenge is not just putting the knowledge into action. The difficulty lies in putting the knowledge into action quickly. In other words, we must learn quickly and apply quickly. Why? Because the whole world is turning into a learning velocity contest. Whether it is business, sports, education, or anything of value, the speed with which we learn has never been more significant. The idea that we can stay the same and not apply new skills is not a possibility anymore.

We see this happen all the time when employees leave companies. Are we going to replace them? Nope. Who is going to do their work? You are.

Who is going to train you? Sally will train you before she leaves… Tomorrow is her last day.

Almost every company we serve has a central challenge that becomes evident when you talk to them about their day-to-day roadblocks… Our people come out of training and still don't know what to do or how to do it. In essence, they are saying that our organizational training and development efforts don't sufficiently build the vital skills that help them add value to growing our business. Why is that? Most training teams simply aren't intentional about overcoming these two learning velocity gaps: The Relevance Gap & The Execution Gap.

The Relevance Gap

In order to overcome the relevance gap, you need to learn to be like a journalist. Journalists are taught to operate from the outside in, and gradually work their way to the top. As a journalist, you are supposed to have several interviews with the people around the situation, so you can bring as much to the final interview as you can. The final interview needs to be with the most important person, which in this case, would be the person you are trying to teach.

The learner needs to understand why these things matter. In order to make this happen, you need to present the geography from two different angles. First, zoom-out as much as you can so they can see the entire map. Second, zoom-in so they can see the exact coordinates. One vantage point provides the big picture perspective, and the other gives them the day-to-day direction. If they don't understand the map from both angles, they won't buy-in to the content you are transferring.

The Execution Gap

What is the execution gap? It simply means that you have transferred content to your audience, and they understand how to apply it in their world... But they don't actually change their behavior to implement the best-practices you've taught them. So, how do we overcome the execution gap? First, we need to pay attention to the distance between the time and place you acquire the knowledge and the time and place you apply the knowledge. Why is this important?

Most of the time, what is taught is rarely applied, which is why most training and development efforts don't work very well. To change that, we need to close the gap between the locus of acquisition and the locus of application. If we deliver training on Friday at ten in the morning, then the participants need to have an assignment to apply this content on that same Friday before two in the afternoon. Then, have them repeat this assignment regularly until you meet again.

Long answer short, if you allow too much time and space between when students are taught, and when they apply, there will be an execution gap. That's why a Digital Training Solution is so valuable. It helps ensure the skills acquired during training are actually being applied.

Anywhere in life, if you want to increase your learning velocity, ask yourself what you are doing to address the relevance gap, and the execution gap. If those gaps aren't being addressed, don't expect your learning speed to increase and don't get mad when you and your team aren't winning the ongoing learning velocity contest.

CHAPTER SUMMARY: LEARNING

First of all, it's hard to pour from an empty cup. If your job as an influencer is to pour yourself out in the service of others, then you won't be able to do that very well if you aren't filled up. That's where learning comes into play.

Secondly, please do not confuse formal education with learning. Valedictorian this and Summa Cum Laude that. None of that really matters, and anyone who has ever completed any degree of higher education knows that the degree is usually a vanity metric for measuring knowledge, skills, and proficiency. I don't say that because I disdain formal education, quite the opposite actually. I loved my MBA experience, but I went into it with a heart to learn as much is I could so I could use it to improve, and ultimately build a successful business. In the end, please remember this...

REAL LEARNING COMES FROM REAL PEOPLE AND REAL-LIFE EXPERIENCES. THUS, YOUR SUCCESS IN LEARNING IS MEASURED BY REAL-LIFE RESULTS.

For example, if you have tons of money and you don't have a home filled with love, you won't fully enjoy the money. Or, if you have a home full of love but you are sick or physically struggling, you won't be able to fully enjoy your loved ones. In sum, learning is always important, but learning the right things is most important. Don't major in the minors.

Third, remember that learning comes in all shapes, sizes, and packages. Some learning happens when we are listening, and some learning happens when we are doing. Some learning comes through questions, and some learning comes through answers... In my experience, the greatest learners have simply become masters at navigating their own psychologies, paradigms, and mindsets.

To become a master of your own psychologies, follow the six best-practices we covered in this chapter:

1. **Unlearn Procurement:** Who you learn from is more important than what they teach you. Stop getting advice from travel agents.

2. **Unlearn Nonsense:** Uncertainty is the driver of most stress and we need to make it make sense if we want to help people change.

3. **Unlearn Acceptance:** When you use a mental model, you won't just blindly believe everything you're told without examining it.

4. **Learn to Learn:** It is hard to pour from an empty cup. A love for reading and writing will help you fill your cup so you can serve.

5. **Learn to Teach:** The teacher learns more than the student, so learn to teach, and teach to learn.

6. **Learn with Velocity:** Knowledge without action is dead. Beat the relevance gap and the execution gap to start winning.

CHAPTER 7

SERVING

"The greatest among you will be your servant."

— Jesus of Nazareth

UNLEARN CONTRIBUTIONS

I was the worst.

It is true. The absolute worst starter on the soccer team.

One season, I played almost every single minute of the entire soccer season (almost 2,000 minutes) and scored only one goal. The goal I scored was an own goal – which, if you don't know what that is, it's not a good thing. To boot, I contributed zero assists. 0.

I challenge you to try to find someone with a less productive "contributions per minutes played" statistic than mine. I'd put my numbers up against anyone who ever played division one college soccer. I don't even know how it is possible to play on a team that was as good as ours (Top 5 Ranking in the Country) and go that many consecutive minutes without accidentally assisting one of your teammates, or at least not scoring for the other team. Believe it or not, they don't measure that type of thing, nor should they. I guess we'll never know.

I say all of that to say this. That same year where I was the worst contributor in the history of contributors, I won an award from the University of Louisville. This award was voted on by the athletic department at UofL and it was called the Cunningham Leadership Award. Each year this award is given to the student-athlete they identify as the most outstanding leader in the Louisville athletic community.

To you, it may not sound like much. But, honestly, I was in a room where I didn't feel like I belonged. Over the years, I got to sit next to Brian Brohm (NFL Quarterback), Peyton Siva (Point Guard in the NBA), Angel McCoughtry (WNBA Superstar), Austin Berry (MLS Rookie of the Year), and many other names that were more recognizable than a kid from Noblesville, Indiana.

When they announced the winner of the award, I thought they made a mistake. I was part of the group that was actually hosting the "Awards Show" and I thought they were calling me up to present an award that I had forgotten to present. I really didn't think that I would be in the top one-hundred vote-getters, let alone the top vote-recipient. I'm not being dramatic.

After sitting there for about ten seconds, they said: Chase, come on up to accept your trophy... I was shocked. I stood up, shook some hands, said thank you, and went back to my seat. I couldn't believe it. Before the night was over, several of the coaches and administrators came to me and said: Thanks for all you've done for our community. Congrats. Well-deserved.

At the end of the night I went home, put my little trophy on my desk and went to sleep. I woke up the next day, called my parents to tell them the good news. I'm pretty sure they were as stunned as I was.

That experience helped me understand that there are two types of moments in life... Moments that make sense, and moments that don't. This moment certainly fell into the latter category. To be honest, there was nothing legendary, historic, or even noteworthy about my athletic career. I never ended up playing professionally, although dozens of my teammates did play in the pros. But for some odd reason, they chose me for that award. And that was the moment in time where I realized that influence is measured by much more than just on-the-field statistics and social media followings. After some intentional reflection, trying to make sense of this experience, I learned a few things...

The Story Behind the Story

Years prior to receiving this award, I realized very quickly that my overall impact as an athlete at the University of Louisville was not going to be measured by tangible impact on the field (if I ever made it onto the field). I realized that if I wanted to leave a mark, and leave the program better off when I left than when I started, I needed to do something significant off the field.

That realization was quite humbling, really. When you finally make it to the Division One level, you realize that everyone else was the best at their high school, and the best on their club team, and the best in their state or their region. So, you quickly go from being the best to being average, or in my case – the worst. Almost everyone gets an unordered slice of humble pie during their freshman year.

How do I make a difference within the program? That opportunity came quickly within my second semester at UofL. All of the athletic teams have to nominate a few members to be what they call SAAC (Student Athlete Advisory Council) Representatives. This is a committee comprised of two to three student-athletes from each team, and they are assembled to provide insight on how to enhance the student-athlete experience. For some reason, I got nominated as a freshman, and every other year after that. Probably because nobody else wanted the extra responsibility.

Within these SAAC requirements, we had what they called Cards Care Competitions, where each athletic team needed to complete a certain amount of community service hours, or conduct simple outreach programs for Louisville Athletics to support the local communities. Instead of just making this a mandate, they made it a competition amongst all the teams, and the winning team received some additional Adidas gear and other goodies of their choosing. In summary, this was the stuff we kept track of to measure our community impact beyond the wins and losses.

From freshman year to senior year, our team logged hundreds of hours of community service and we won all kinds of awards for our commitment to serving the community. We really did a great job of serving those in the Louisville area.

So where do I come into play? I was just the guy that that had the privilege of organizing all of our team's community service initiatives. I guess because I was the organizer, I felt like it would have been hypocritical of me if I didn't attend and help lead the projects. I don't know how many community service hours I logged in my four years, but it was a lot. I was a regular at some of the local Boys and Girls Clubs and nearby homeless shelters and food pantries. All that to say this, the stuff we did off the field (over the years) started to add up, and I guess a few people started to notice.

After several hours of concentrated introspection, I came to the conclusion that I still didn't deserve this award – but I did finally realize the yardstick that was used for measuring true leadership...

LEADERSHIP IS SIMPLY INFLUENCE.
INFLUENCE IS MEASURED BY IMPACT.
TRUE IMPACT HAPPENS WHEN YOU SERVE.

UNLEARN SERVANT LEADERSHIP

I don't believe in servant leadership. There is no such thing. It is just simply called leadership. What do leaders do? We serve. That's the crux of what we do.

The best place to go for context on this idea is to look at the one that many people call the most influential person to ever walk on the planet.

Here is a paraphrasing of some of the text, with my updated version of what it might sound like in today's language:

> *You know that the worldly rulers, the CEOs, and the Top-Level Executives, the people in charge of governments – they often use authority, force, coercion, control, and domination to lead their people. They pretend to be superior.*
>
> *But it shouldn't be this way. Truly, whoever wishes to become great among you should become your servant.*
>
> *Whoever wants to be the best and succeed at the highest level will be a servant to many.*
>
> *I did not come to be served, but to serve, and to give my life as a sacrifice for many. If you want to achieve greatness, I suggest you think about doing the same thing.*[1]

So, what do leaders and influencers do? The great ones serve.

UNLEARN LIMITATIONS

> *"There is no man living who isn't capable of doing more than he thinks he can do."* – Henry Ford

Great quote... But at what moment do we discover that we are capable of more?

December 24th. We were drinking eggnog and enjoying our traditional Christmas Eve Celebration at My Grandma and Grandpa's home in Pierceton, Indiana. Suzanne and I were married and had our sweet Lael. It must have been 2015 or 2016, because Evie wasn't born yet.

I'm sitting in Grandpa's wooden rocking chair in the corner of the dining room with Lael crying in my arms and right next to my Aunt Susan. For the first time, I asked her, "How did you and Uncle Greg make it all work when you had Ryan?"

In the midst of several miscarriages and different challenges, they had Holly and Jill, who are two of my favorite cousins. Then they had their third child, Ryan, who side-hustles as a real-life superhero. He was born with something called Apert Syndrome which exists in about .0005 percent of newborn babies.[2]

When you meet Ryan, the first thing you'll notice about him is how amazing he is. Kind, generous, selfless, and always helping others. The next question you might ask yourself is: How does he do it all?

Ryan has a full-time job. He probably has more money in his savings account than many fifty-year-old men. He has his driver's license. He has many friends. He has been on several mission trips to various countries. He is an active member at his church and within his small-town Indiana community. And, he has supernaturally endured 52 different surgeries.

Add it all up, and you can start to see how fascinating this story is.

Then factor in that he doesn't have elbows. When he was born, his fingers were fused together and his feet were webbed. He can't see very much without glasses or hear very well without hearing aids.

No problem, right?

I said, NO ELBOWS! He literally can't bend his arms.

Stop what you are doing for just a minute and try to feed yourself without bending your elbows. Now try to wash your hair. Now try to brush your teeth. Now try to put on your glasses. Now try to put on your hearing aids. Now try putting on all your clothes. Now try cleaning your ears. Wash your face. Tie your shoes.

How'd that go?

You starting to see how incredible this story is?

Back to the original question and why I asked my Aunt Susan... "How did you and Uncle Greg make it all work when you had Ryan?"

"You just do it. You do what you need to do. You make the necessary sacrifices and you just find a way and you do your best. It is not always easy, but God gives you everything you need."

All that said, watching my Aunt Susan and the amount of "stuff" she accomplishes on a daily basis is just flat-out inspiring... Here's an incomplete list: She works full time as a Nurse Manager (in Pediatrics ICU, which is highly stressful), and takes great care of my Grandma (who has Alzheimer's). Babysits all of her grandchildren, often. Tends a world-class garden and uses the fruit of her labor to cook delicious homemade meals. Sends me and all my kids homemade cards on every occasion. Organizes Christmas, Thanksgiving, and all major family get togethers. Remembers every birthday, and every anniversary. Active member at her church. Knits clothes, scarves, blankets, hats and shawls. Sews anything and everything. Her and my Uncle Greg own a successful small business and they own a real estate investment property. They serve on boards. They give generously to charities. This list could go on and on.

I've watched them do jaw-droppingly amazing things over the decades, and their momentum just seemed to keep going even after Ryan started to grow older and became more self-sufficient. When we stop and truly reflect on the power of this story, it leads me to wonder how it is possible that many of us feel like we are already busy and incapable of doing more?

I remember when Suzanne and I lived in Louisville, we were a part of this awesome church small group that would meet every Sunday evening at the Brizendine's home. We were newlyweds with no kids and no "real" responsibilities and yet we were the only ones who never really brought any food or snacks to the gathering. All of the other families with several kids made these homemade meals and yet we were somehow too "busy" to make anything so we stopped at the grocery store on the way to pick up a 2-liter and a bag of chips.

How did we deceive ourselves into thinking we were busy? No kids. Didn't own a company at the time... What were we busy doing? I'm bringing this all to light as more of an after-thought to watching this entire story unfold before my eyes. First of all, when we witness something truly inspirational like this, we should honor these heroes in our lives and share their stories. Secondly, we should reflect on their stories and learn as much as possible so we can use these life-lessons to help more people.

For now, the deepest message I've uncovered from the reflection is this... When you know other people are depending on you, there are no more sick days. When you realize that someone else needs you, there is no more lying in bed until noon. You get out of bed and do what needs to be done.

This realization is one of the greatest inherent gifts that comes with being a good parent. Same thing with owning a business. What if I am sick and don't feel like I am able to get out of bed to process the paychecks for my team? Get out of bed. Their families are depending on you. I better find a way to sign the front of those checks so their kids have diapers.

The momentum that is created by this "I am responsible for the wellbeing of another human being" mindset can help you discover the path to your true potential.

And, in this story, I'm not sure who helped who more. Did Ryan help Susan more or did Susan help Ryan more? Was it the chicken or the egg?

So, let's all be more like Ryan and Susan. Be the type of person that other people can depend on – everyday, and you'll start to get a glimpse of your true capabilities.

LEARN TO MAXIMIZE VALUE

When true influencers recognize what they are capable of, the next logical thing to do is to acquire a non-profit business model mindset. Before acquiring a non-profit business model mindset, we have to overcome the status game mindset.

What is status? It is your ranking in the social ecosystem. When we play status games, we seek to find out who is number one and who is number two in the hierarchy... But who really cares?

There are several problems with status games... Here are two of them:

1. Who decides on your ranking?
2. To be the winner, there has to be a loser.

Quit wasting your life playing status games. When you "win" you really don't win anything, and they ultimately militate against the true meaning of success (true success doesn't create losers).

Success is more often found when you help other people get what they want...

The Typical Success Journey:

> Part 1: When first starting out on the journey towards success, most people try to win status games because they think they will be a catalyst for them.

Part 2: Then, at some point, you realize that the only catalyst to the destination of success is to help others be successful.

Part 3: When you finally find the destination of success, you want to help a lot of people find the destination, too.

Conclusion: The more successful you become, the more you seek to help others be successful, and the more successful you become...

SKIP THE STATUS GAMES AND JUST GO HELP PEOPLE

I learned about this important concept when I was in Graduate School in November of 2012. It was our last class before Thanksgiving break and I was sitting in the back row of my Managerial Economics class. My favorite graduate school teacher, Dr. Durso, walked into the room and asked... Why do organizations exist?

Someone in our class raised their hand and said to maximize profit, which was the correct answer according to the textbook. Within a few seconds, I raised my hand from the back of the room and asked...

Chase: I guess for-profit institutions probably exist for that reason, but what about non-profits, why do they exist? In their names, it states pretty clearly that profit is not the ultimate objective.

Dr. Durso: That's an excellent question, let's talk about that.

At the time, I was the President of the Board of Directors for a Non-Profit Ministry in Louisville and was also a Board Member for another small Non-Profit organization. This was intriguing to me, mainly because I helped manage the books for the one ministry, and it sure didn't seem like we were in existence to make much of a profit.

She opened the conversation up to the class.

Dr. Durso: What do you think class? Why do non-profits exist?

Chase: Maybe to maximize benefit or maximize blessing or *maximize the value* they bring to the people they serve?

Dr. Durso: I think you are exactly right. If money isn't the main driver, then their main driver for existence is probably to help their audience, bless their audience, bring benefit or value to their audience without a focus on money as a primary outcome.

Dr. Durso was a fantastic teacher, and she was great at opening our eyes to how businesses can be forces for good in this world. When it comes to influence, we all need the non-profit mindset of maximizing value, or maximizing benefit, or maximizing blessing. In my little corner of the universe, I have found that when we focus more on serving people, and less on profitability, the more profitable we seem to become. Ironic?

In the end, I guess if you help enough people get what they want, you'll end up getting what you want...

LEARN TO MAKE THEM MISS YOU

How will we know when we've helped people get what they want? I learned how to measure this in October of 2018. I don't remember the exact day but I'll never forget the events of the day. It was seven-something in the morning when this happened:

Ring... Bev.
Ring... Mike.
Ring... Jason.
Ring... Kelly.
Ring... Amanda.
Ring... Shannon.
Ring... Bridgett.

Bev: What are we going to do?

Chase: Hold on a sec my friend, Kelly is calling. Let me tell her I'm on the phone with you.

Chase: Hey Kelly, I'm on the phone with Bev can I call you right back?

Kelly: What are we going to do?

Chase: Hold tight for just a minute I promise I'll call you right back after I get off the phone with Bev.

Ring. Ring. Ring. I spent the next few weeks playing the role of a severely underpaid psychologist, talking dozens of people off the "I need to find a new job" ledge. Why was everyone in such disarray? Before I tell you why, let me take you back to February of 2017 when my friend Granville and I flew down to Arizona to support two of his leadership teams in the Phoenix area. When I walked in the door, the first people I met were Jason and Tsera...

Jason: "Hey welcome to the family, Chase. Thanks for coming down. If Granville says you're alright, that's all we need to know. You're one of us now."

Chase: "That's very kind, thank you for the warm welcome. That's cool to hear about your respect for Granville. How long have you guys been working together?"

Tsera: "Several years... In fact, there is no way I would even be a leader without Granville. He stuck his neck out for me and gave me the opportunity and the confidence to be a leader. I would have never even applied if it weren't for him. The rest is history, so they say."

Chase: "How about you, Jason?"

Jason: "Same thing. Granville's family. Sometimes they forget about us down here in Arizona, but not Granville. He has always had our backs and fights for us. Always checking on us to make sure we have everything we need and lets us know how important we are to the team. I told Granville, wherever he goes, he's going to have to take me with him."

Back to all the phone calls on that October morning. Not long before the calls started coming in, Granville announced he was leaving the department to take his talent to another team. Some of them went with him. Some of them would have rather waited in the unemployment line, and that's not a joke.

What are we going to do now that Granville is taking his talent somewhere else? They asked with trepidation. Should I look for a new job? Are you hiring? What if so and so gets the job, there is no way I could ever work for so and so...

Growing up in the 90's, I remember Michael Jordan saying: "I'm not playing for anyone other than Phil Jackson." I thought that was a bit crazy of MJ, and I didn't know that kind of loyalty existed in the real world with real people... Until Granville announced his upcoming departure. This type of commitment is rare to see in the business world and is typically only seen within the family construct.

What I am about to tell you is probably an unfair generalization of people, but I believe it to be true... Most people don't care about people. They care about what the people do for them. In the wise words of Jack Butcher:

"WE DON'T VALUE THE THING, WE VALUE OUR RELATIONSHIP TO THE THING."

Similarly, people don't value the widget they purchased, they value what the widget does for them. We generally don't value the person. We value our relationship to the person. So, what did Granville do for so many people?

Call after call after call I got to hear the same story from several different voices. He was the security blanket for them. He made them feel safe. He protected them. They felt secure. Subtract Granville and you subtract all of those feelings of comfort. Then adrenaline kicks in and they go into fight or flight mode, or even full-on survival mode. Remember, uncertainty is the driver of most stress. He was their certainty. He was predictable. He was safe.

I've travelled all over America with Granville. We've been to Reds games (I got my first foul ball with him), and NKU basketball games. We've been to funerals together. I've met over one-thousand people that worked for him. I know his family and he knows mine. His Uncle even built the apps for Maximize Value. His wife has been to my seminars. I've been to his daughter's dance events.

What do you say about someone like that? Probably something similar to what Jason said during our first conversation.

Tie this whole story back to influence and we can be convinced of this… Perhaps the greatest indicator of your success in maximizing influence lies in the answer to this question:

WILL THEY MISS YOU WHEN YOU'RE GONE?

Serve them in such a way that they miss you when you're gone.

LEARN WELL DONE GOOD & FAITHFUL

Back to where we started this journey in the first chapter, I am again reminded of a moment from August, 2012. I found myself sitting in our living room with five of my Grandparents (all four of my Grandparents and one of my Great Grandmas).

"It's not supposed to happen like this. No parent is supposed to bury their child. It's supposed to be the other way around." – Grandpa Duggins

At that moment in time, I came face to face with the harsh reality that life on this earth could end sooner than expected. We all think we know this truth until we spend a night in the morgue and realize that this tent is really just a tent.

After that experience, I bought hundreds of these little blue wristbands with one word on them: LEGACY (a thing handed down by a predecessor).

In relation to a legacy, I have a pretty clear idea about how God has used me to help companies all over the world to make millions and millions of dollars. I saw more money pass through my hands before I turned thirty than many people will see in their entire lifetime. I say that with tremendous humility and gratitude.

I know I've had a substantial impact in my little corner of the marketplace, far more than I ever thought I would at this age. But, as I sit down and confront the reality of death, it is interesting to see how unimportant some of those things are when you zoom out to look at the big picture.

When I make time to think about this reality, it always brings me back to this quote from Francis Chan:

> **"OUR GREATEST FEAR SHOULD NOT BE OF FAILURE BUT OF SUCCEEDING AT THINGS IN LIFE THAT DON'T REALLY MATTER."**

From my angle, it is vanity to worry about prominence or riches. Don't worry about your net worth or how recognizable your name is. In fact, once you become more popular or more recognizable – you'll probably wish you would have kept a lower profile by helping people more anonymously (just ask Michael Jordan about the price of fame).

If you are going to worry about anything, worry about how well you love people. How well you prioritize people. How well you serve people. Worry about the depth with which you impact the individuals you get to help. Worry about living according to the truth, and sharing it with those you love. Worry about how you positively influence the people in your life.

My final recommendation is to think about the metric by which your life will be judged, and make a commitment to live every day so that in the end, you'll hear these words:

WELL DONE, GOOD AND FAITHFUL SERVANT

CHAPTER SUMMARY: SERVING

Why is it that we have a natural tendency to honor and respect those who sacrificed themselves for the good of others? Why don't we have a problem bowing in appreciation to those who surrendered their own agendas in order to be a part of something bigger than themselves?

BECAUSE WHEN SELFISHNESS IS EVERYWHERE, SELFLESSNESS IS COMPELLING.

In the end, our winning percentage as influencers will increase when we are selfless enough to consistently pour ourselves out in the service of others.

In order to be better servants, let's apply the six core messages from this chapter:

1. **Unlearn Contributions:** Leadership is influence. Influence is measured by impact. True impact happens when you serve.

2. **Unlearn Servant Leadership:** You can't be a true leader without serving... And the greatest among you will be your servant.

3. **Unlearn Limitations:** Be a person that other people can depend on and you'll start to get a glimpse of your true potential.

4. **Learn to Maximize Value:** When it comes to influence, we all need the non-profit mindset of serving people as much as we can.

5. **Learn to Make Them Miss You:** The greatest indicator of your influence: WILL THEY MISS YOU WHEN YOU'RE GONE?

6. **Learn Well Done Good & Faithful:** In the end, make sure you hear: WELL DONE GOOD AND FAITHFUL SERVANT.

WE ARE HERE

"You can't get better unless you get started."

– Jack Butcher

We are here.

We made it this far, and in the wise words of Dr. Seuss, I must say:

> *"Congratulations!*
> *Today is your day.*
> *You're off to Great Places!*
> *You're off and away!*
> *You have brains in your head.*
> *You have feet in your shoes.*
> *You can steer yourself any direction you choose."*

I agree with all of that, but I must stop the quote at that exact point. Why? Because I don't agree with the next part of the story. It says *you're on your own...* Which I don't believe to be true.

I said WE are here, because I don't believe you are doing this life on your own, and I know for certain I'm not on my own.

After reading these pages, you found a book that is full of personal stories. That was intentional because I wanted to tell people about the unknown heroes I've been blessed to befriend along the way. There isn't much talk about celebrities or famous athletes in this book. Some of those stories are fantastic and some aren't. But they are widely told.

Instead, I know some real heroes that aren't famous and probably never will be. But they are heroes to me, and their stories deserve to be shared. They inspired me, and if you considered this book from the right heart posture, I am sure these heroes inspired you, too.

Back to the point. I believe everyone can be a hero, and unfortunately, some just aren't.

At least not yet.

I'm not sure why some people live a heroic life, and some never tap into their potential. Perhaps it is because they don't know exactly where to start. So, I would like to help you with that. Start simple and start with yourself.

A life of influencing others starts with learning to influence yourself. We can find a good starting point by looking at the things we do every single day. Those are some of the most important actions in your life (basic math) because your day is a microcosm of your life. If you want to influence your life more effectively, you have to influence the things you do every day. Start by selecting one thing and making it better. Rinse and repeat tomorrow. Let's keep doing this every day, and eventually we will find that we were able to successfully clean up some of our own messes, and naturally we'll have the confidence to start helping other people clean up some of their messes, too.

That may sound trivial to you. It may sound too simple or too common to be helpful. But unfortunately, after traveling the world to help people, I know for certain that common knowledge is not always common practice. The idea I have given you is just as true as it sounds and just as simple as it seems. We can put it to the acid test if we'd like, but when we've completed the examination, we'll find real gold.

Final Thoughts

I've given myself to this journey in hopes that *you* would find at least one idea inside that *influences* you to be a better you. This book was written with you in mind. And with gratitude, I humbly say THANK YOU.

I appreciate you picking up this book and reading these words. I'm better because of you, and I know that to be true. And we are better together.

One last reminder (from Paul of Tarsus)…

"LET'S NOT GET TIRED OF DOING WHAT IS GOOD, FOR AT THE RIGHT TIME WE WILL REAP A HARVEST IF WE DO NOT GIVE UP."

NOTES

Chapter 1:

1. Bible, Crossway. "The Parable of the Talents". *English Standard Version* (Matthew 25: 14 – 30) Wheaton, III.: Crossway Bible, 2016.
2. Eurich, Tasha. "Increase your self- awareness with one simple fix." November, 2017. TED.com.
3. Berkshire Hathaway. 2004. "Morning Session - 2004 Meeting." *CNBC*. May 1, 2004. https://buffett.cnbc.com/video/2004/05/01/morning-session---2004-berkshire-hathaway-annual-meeting.html.
4. Campbell, Angus. *The Sense of Well-Being in America: Recent Patterns and Trends.* 23 Aug 2007. McGraw-Hill, 1981.

Chapter 2:

1. Heath, Dan. *Upstream: The Quest to Solve Problems Before They Happen.* New York, NY 10020: AVID READER PRESS An Imprint of Simon & Schuster, Inc, 1230 Avenue of Americas, 2020.
2. "The Eisenhower Matrix: Introduction & 3-Minute Video Tutorial." *Eisenhower*, February 7, 2017. https://www.eisenhower.me/eisenhower-matrix/.
3. Covey, Stephen. *The 7 Habits of Highly Effective People.* First Edition. Free Press, 1989.
4. Hummel, Charles. *The Tyranny of the Urgent.* As a booklet by InterVarsity Press, 1984.
5. Accident description in the Aviation Safety Network's Aviation Safety Database, http://aviation-safety.net/database
6. Koch, Richard. *The 80/20 Principle.* 1998. London: Nicholas Brealey Publishing.
7. "Every Dollar." Ramsey Solutions. https://www.ramseysolutions.com/ramseyplus/everydollar.

Chapter 3:

1. Mineo, Liz. "Over Nearly 80 Years, Harvard Study Has Been Showing How to Live a Healthy and Happy Life." Harvard Gazette. November 26, 2018.
2. Waldinger, Robert. "What Makes a Good Life? Lessons from the Longest Study on Happiness." TED.
3. Solan, Matthew. "The Secret to Happiness? Here's Some Advice from the Longest-Running Study on Happiness." Harvard Health, October 5, 2017.
4. Vaillant, George. "Keys to a Healthy Retirement." Harvard Business Review. August 21, 2014. https://hbr.org/2009/04/keys-to-a-healthy-retirement.
5. Curtin, Melanie. "This 75-Year Harvard Study Found the 1 Secret to Leading a Fulfilling Life." Inc.com. Inc., February 27, 2017. https://www.inc.com/melanie-curtin/want-a-life-of-fulfillment-a-75-year-harvard-study-says-to-prioritize-this-one-t.html.
6. Dreamer, Oriah Mountain. "The Invitation." 1999. http://www.oriahmountaindreamer.com/.
7. Cates, Sean. *Father & Son.* Victory. Amazon.com, 2015.

Chapter 4:

1. "Yad Vashem Holocaust Museum." yadvashem.org. https://www.yadvashem.org
2. "People Pleasing: Short-Term Benefits and Long-Term Costs." *Psychology Today.* https://www.psychologytoday.com/us/blog/light-and-shadow/201409/people-pleasing-short-term-benefits-and-long-term-costs
3. "Sociotropy-autonomy and situation-specific anxiety." Toru Sotu, Doug McCann, Cristen Ferguson-Isaac. https://pubmed.ncbi.nlm.nih.gov/15077750/
4. Van Edwards, Vanessa. *Captivate, The Science of Succeeding with People. Kindle ed.* Penguin Random House. 2017.
5. Heath, Dan, and Chip Heath. *Made to Stick.* "Elizabeth Newton: Tappers and Listeners". The Random House Publishing Group, 2007.

Chapter 5:

1. Lewin, Kurt (1936). Principles of Topological Psychology. New York: McGraw-Hill.
2. Weingarten, Gene. "Pearls Before Breakfast: Can One of the Nation's Great Musicians Cut through the Fog of a D.C. Rush Hour? Let's Find out." The Washington Post. April 8, 2007.
3. Olsen, Jeff. *The Slight Edge*. First Edition. Success, 2005.
4. Liu, Evie. "McDonald's and Other Fast Food Chains Should Keep an Eye on Chick-Fil-A". Barrons. June 10, 2019. https://www.barrons.com/articles/mcdonalds-has-a-real-competitor-in-chick-fil-a-51560162600.
5. "The Only Home of Throwed Rolls - Sikeston, MO: Ozark, MO: Foley, AL." Lambert's Cafe. https://throwedrolls.com/.

Chapter 6:

1. Maxwell, John C. *The 5 Levels of Leadership. Kindle ed. Center Street*, 2011.
2. Bowden, Mark. "*The Dark Art of Interrogation.*" The Atlantic. Atlantic Media Company, October 2003 Issue. https://www.theatlantic.com/magazine/archive/2003/10/the-dark-art-of-interrogation/302791/
3. Weiner, Tim. *The Spy Agency's Many Mean Ways to Loosen Cold-War Tongues. The New York Times*, February 9, 1997. https://www.nytimes.com/1997/02/09/weekinreview/the-spy-agency-s-many-mean-ways-to-loosen-cold-war-tongues.html
4. Maslow, Abraham H. *A Theory of Human Motivation*. 1943. General Press, 2013.
5. Scarlett, Hilary. *Neuroscience for Organizational Change: An Evidence-Based Practical Guide to Managing Change.* Kogan Page, 2016.
6. Greaves, Jean, and Travis Bradberry. *Emotional Intelligence 2.0*. New Edition. San Diego, CA 92121, 11526 Sorrento Valley Road: Talent Smart, 2009.
7. Matthew. "A Warning Against Hypocrisy" *The Holy Bible, New International Version*, (Matthew 23:15) 2011. Biblica (formerly International Bible Society).
8. Hollins, Peter. *Mental Models: 30 Thinking Tools That Separate the Average From the Exceptional. Improved Decision-Making, Logical Analysis, and Problem-Solving.* Kindle. PH Learning Inc., 2019.
9. Zeelenberg, Marcel, and Kees van den Bos. "The Inaction Effect in the Psychology of Regret." ResearchGate. Marcel Zeelenberg, April 2002.
10. "Grant Cardone Keynote - Training Technologies". Grant Cardone Training Technologies. https://store.grantcardone.com
11. Jordon, Steve. "Investors Earn Handsome Paychecks by Handling Buffett's Business." *Omaha World-Herald*, April 28, 2013.
12. Matthew. "The Narrow Way." *The Holy Bible, New International Version*, (Matthew 7:13-14) 2011. Biblica (formerly International Bible Society).
13. Loehr, Jim, and Tony Schwartz. *The Power of Full Engagement*. 1230 Avenue of the Americas, New York, NY 10020. The Free Press, A Division of Simon & Schuster, Inc. 2003.
14. Mueller, Pam A. Essay. In *The Pen Is Mightier Than the Keyboard: Advantages of Longhand Over Laptop Note Taking*, edited by Daniel M. Oppenheimer. Psychological Science, 2014.
15. Graham, S., and Hebert, M. A. (2010). Writing to Read: Evidence for How Writing Can Improve Reading. A Carnegie Corporation Time to Act Report. Washington, DC: Alliance for Excellent Education.
16. James. "Faith and Deeds." *The Holy Bible, New International Version*, (James 2:14-18) 2011. Biblica (formerly International Bible Society).

Chapter 7:

1. Mark. "Serving." *The Holy Bible, New International Version*, (Mark 10:42-45) 2011. Biblica (formerly International Bible Society).
2. "Apert Syndrome: Symptoms, Treatment, and Prognosis." Medical News Today. MediLexicon International. https://www.medicalnewstoday.com/articles/320907.

ABOUT THE AUTHOR

I love God. I love my beautiful wife. I love my three energetic kids. I love my family and friends. I love America. I love sports (golf, basketball, soccer, snow skiing, wakeboarding). I love my Louisville Cardinals.

I am thankful for our Maximize Value team and all the people around the world that we get to serve.

God bless you and thank you for letting me be a part of your journey.

Every Friday, I send out a free inspirational email to thousands of people. If you would like to be included, please join us by visiting:

CHASEKREGER.COM

ABOUT MAXIMIZE VALUE

We are the corporate training team that provides the enthusiasm and the insight you need to stay motivated. You can trust us to challenge the status quo and deliver measurable results.

How could your team benefit from partnering with us?

1. **Assessments:** We start our partnership with a pre-training assessment which helps us create a targeted action plan completely customized to the growth needs of your team. This allows our partners to truly pinpoint where to allocate the development resources.

2. **Dynamic, Live, Face-to-Face Facilitation:** Lecture? Far from it. Traditional training? Not at all. Engaging? Absolutely! Thought provoking? You better believe it. And, with respect to our current world, we also offer live, virtual training options.

3. **Ongoing Digital Training:** Even after a transformational development experience, routine maintenance is still necessary. That's where our digital video training platform comes into play…To ensure the skills acquired during training are being applied.

MAXIMIZEVALUE.COM

ADDITIONAL RESOURCES

Digital Training Courses: maximizevaluedigital.com ($99 - $499)

Maximize Influence Digital Course 50% Off Code: MIFOR$99

Free iPhone & iPad App: Maximize Value (App Store)

Free Android App: Maximize Value (Google Play Store)

Free Leadership & Sales Assessments: mvassessments.com

Free Inspirational Videos: maximizevalue.com/videos

Free Bonus Chapter: chasekreger.com/bonus

Free Book Resources: chasekreger.com/books

Audio Book: chasekreger.com/books

Questions: ckreger@maximizevalue.com

WE HAVE TWO OPTIONS

INFLUENCED

OR

INFLUENCER

WHICH ONE ARE YOU?